GROWING LEADERS

A DEFINITIVE GUIDE

All rights reserved © 2024 - Vidusha Nathavitharana
Editorial consultant: Dr. Devika Brendon
Initially published by JAMFRUIT PUBLISHERS in 2020

This book is sold to the condition that it shall not, by war of trade or otherwise, be lent, re-sold, hired out, copied, extensively quoted or otherwise circulated, in any from of binding or cover other than which it is published, without the express written permission of the author. Content contained or made available through this book is not intended to constitute legal advice or financial advice, and no attorney-client relationship is formed through this published work. No part of this book may be reproduced or transmitted in any form or by any means, electronic or mechanical, including photocopying, recording or by any information storage and retrieval system, without written permission from the authors, except for the inclusion of brief quotations in a review.

Disclaimer: The practices of the Liberation Tigers of Tamil Eelam (LTTE) are referenced in this book as an illustrative example. This reference does not imply any affinity, affiliation, commendation, or partisanship towards any party involved in the Sri Lankan civil war. This work does not endorse war or violence and acknowledges the profound loss and destruction that war inflicts upon a nation and its people.

Limit of Liability Disclaimer: The information provided in this book is for informational purposes only and is not intended to be a source of direct consulting with respect to the material presented. The publisher and the authors do not make any guarantee or other promise as to any results that may be obtained from using the content in this book.. To the maximum extent permitted by law, the publisher and the authors disclaim any and all liability in the event any information, commentary, analysis, opinions, advice and/or recommendations contained in this book prove to be inaccurate, incomplete, unreliable, or result in any type of loss.

Earnings Disclaimer: All income examples in this book are examples. They are not intended to represent or guarantee that everyone will achieve the same results.

Published by:

Growing Leaders - 1st Edition. 2024
ASIN: B0D9F3GS76 (Amazon Kindle)
ISBN: 978-1-923223-26-4 (eBook)
ISBN: 978-1-923223-27-1(Amazon Paperback)
ISBN: 978-1-923223-28-8 (Amazon Hardcover)
ISBN: 978-1-923223-29-5 (Ingram Spark Paperback)
ISBN: 978-1-923223-30-1 (Ingram Spark Hardcover)
ISBN: 978-1-923223-26-4 (Smashwords)

TRADEMARKS
All product names, logos, and brands are the property of their respective owners. All company, product, and service names used in this book are for identification purposes only. Using these names, logos, and brands does not imply endorsement. All other trademarks cited herein are the property of their respective owners.

GROWING LEADERS

A DEFINITIVE GUIDE

With foreword from Dave Ulrich, the Father of Modern HR

VIDUSHA NATHAVITHARANA

Dedicated to my Aththa[1], who proudly tilled the land, and fathered strong-willed and values-driven children: one of whom became the man who nurtured me...

1 Grandfather

Foreword

Google 'Leader' with 6.4 billion results and 'Leadership' with 10.4 billion results! Obviously, the study of Leaders and Leadership continues to matter, with about as many comments as there are people on Earth (7.9 billion, 2021).

So, why another book and what does Vidusha's work uniquely provide?

Why?

Clearly, Leadership matters. Everyone can quickly point to a Leader who enriched and a Leader who impoverished their personal and professional lives. Research confirms personal experience. At work, effective Leaders inspire and motivate their followers; create organisations that offer products and services that customers value; and increase confidence for investors and communities.

Yet, much of the research shows a dearth of Leadership: as employee confidence and trust in Leaders falls, as Leadership tenure gets shorter, and as succession pools of qualified Leaders for key positions get smaller,

Most of us know that Leadership matters and have personal ideas on how to be a better Leader, yet personal Leadership progress is slow, and building Leadership depth is often wanting.

What?

Into this thicket, Vidusha offers insightful and useful advice on how to be a better Leader and build better Leadership.

His focus is on how to grow a future Leader, using the metaphor of farming and growing crops. Farmers don't just plant and then sit idly by, hoping their "paddy cultivation" (his word) will grow. He brings into this work wonderful insights from his personal experiences and organisations where he has helped Leaders grow, particularly in Sri Lanka.

Leaders are both born with natural predispositions and bred with learning competencies (about 50/50). His focus on the four phases of growing Leaders helps develop the learning competencies of Leaders.

1. Preparing the soil. The context or setting for upgrading Leaders requires attention to mindset, framework, and resources. Leadership development begins before Leaders engage in their development.
2. Planting. Identifying the predispositions of individuals to lead, and helping those who aspire to improve recognise how to do so, plants the seeds of Leadership.

3. Nurturing and watching over. Investing in Leadership comes in many forms, including training, work experience, job assignments, coaching, mentoring, and personal learning.
4. Harvesting. Managing a Leadership career includes attention to succession, mobility, retention, and ultimately retirement.

For each of these four phases of "growing" Leaders, we are given specific tips to consider, checklists to evaluate, and stories to illustrate.

I am especially drawn to Vidusha's compelling stories where he goes beyond superficial journalism, to report the specific and relevant actions by leading organisations to grow their Leaders. The tools come alive as they are demonstrated with examples.

Some key messages include that growing Leaders is not a quick fix (gestation for plants takes time), requires personalised attention (one size does not fit all), improves by weaving together many separate initiatives into an integrated system (there is no magic Leadership development bullet), and can be done (and is worth the effort!).

By the end of this thoughtful work, Vidusha has created an incredible menu (keeping with the food metaphor) of outstanding ideas that will grow Leaders and Leadership. Anyone who wants to be a better Leader or build better Leadership can select the menu item (Leadership tip, tool, and action) and quickly apply it to make progress.

Vidusha can clearly be called an accomplished cultivator of Leaders!

Dave Ulrich
Rensis Likert Professor, Ross School of Business,
University of Michigan
Partner, The RBL Group
dou@umich.edu
Alpine, Utah

CONTENTS

Prologue

My paternal Grandparents' clan were farmers. The vocation continues to this date, with large tracts of paddy cultivation still taking place with relatively low mechanisation and industrialisation. Though there is a clear focus on the yield and the harvest, there is a bigger focus on the quality of the produce and its 'fit' for consumption.

My Grandparents' generation was the first to be introduced to chemical fertilisers, pesticides, and weedicides. Many adopted these and were able to generate much larger harvests. However, many in my Grandfather's clan were wary of these 'chemicals' and warned that they would have long-term repercussions, not only for those who consumed them but for the environment overall.

Their rather obstinate refusal to use anything chemical made no sense at the time, but makes all the sense in the world now; and with all the major health issues and environmental impacts now being keenly observed, their wisdom to not allow short-term gain to destroy long-term health must be both admired, and learnt from.

'You can't demand plants to grow faster, you can only love and nurture them,' was something they would collectively tell anyone who came to 'sell' the 'chemical'. Even when some organisations offered it to them for free, they did not try it out. 'It is not about the money,' they would often tell them, 'it is about the harm it does.' Watching the little fish in the streams die, the waterways getting polluted and many 'strange' illnesses taking place around the village, my Grandparents' clan brought everyone together and made a pact that their lands would never use anything apart from organic produce for their fields; a tradition that continues to date, for the most part.

'You can't demand plants to grow faster' is something that stuck with me. We almost always want things to happen according to our time. We want immediate results. We want to be able to control the output. This is near impossible with plants. You must give it time. You can certainly do Research and Development, and find out better varieties and methods but, bottom line, the plant will grow when the plant grows, all we can do is to do our part to facilitate that. We are not influencing the plant, we are influencing its environment, and giving the plant everything it needs to bring about its fullest potential. The plant knows how to grow; you do not need to tell it that. All it needs is the right setting.

Many years later, this analogy came to mind when we were trying to look at Leadership development initiatives for clients that we were working with. Many organisations look at developing and grooming Leaders as a 'Programmatic' approach, rather than a holistic, interlinked and long-term process. Investing resources towards conducting cutting-edge training Programs never quite helps in developing a Leader, simply because learning to lead is something each individual will go about slightly differently. Simply herding them all to a retreat and expecting them to come out of it as 'Leaders' is simply wishful thinking.

Plants don't grow on demand; neither do Leaders.

Rather than taking a mechanical approach to developing Leaders within an organisation, I think it is far more practical, and wise, to look at the concept of 'growing' Leaders rather than 'making Leaders.' It takes a village to raise a child; it takes the entire organisation to build a Leader. Leadership development is not something that can be done in isolation. Nor can it be done in a hurry. If you go down this route, it almost always ends up with sub-optimal Leaders in the longer term.

Needless to say, growing Leadership pipelines and having a healthy mix of Leaders at all levels is a critical necessity for any organisation. Leaders are the heartbeat of the organisation, and without them, an organisation will not be able to successfully navigate the many challenges it will face, and will have an untimely death.

Great organisations are created rarely because of chance; they almost always exist because of great Leaders.

The aim of this book is to take a deep and detailed look at how organisations can grow Leaders within their fold. Using the ancient South Asian practice of paddy cultivation to offer conceptual insights and analogies, the book also looks at novel and often uncelebrated practices from both mainstream and outlier organisations, in order to offer practical tips and hacks. The book takes the lifecycle of paddy cultivation and weaves the development of Leaders around it. Each chapter is both a stand-alone section, as well as part of the whole. I advise reading it from the start, so that the interconnections are not lost. However, if it is a few particular aspects that you want to read first, each chapter will offer context and clarity as a stand-alone entity, as well.

Part 1

Preparing the Soil

Traditional paddy cultivation in Sri Lanka still exists. It is a ritualistic and reverent undertaking, almost never practiced for the sole purpose of profiting from it. Traditional communities still grow paddy for their own consumption first, and they sell only the surplus (which, till very recently, there almost always was).

It was also very much a collective exercise. There was a plot that belonged to everyone collectively, and the entire clan got involved in cultivating it. There was no 'singular' ownership of paddy lands until much later. Fathers passed it on to their children, and they generally tilled the land in return, and it got passed down from generation to generation. There were no slaves in Sri Lanka at any point in its history, and all Sri Lankans were 'free men' who were segregated in class structure based on their vocation, and these vocations were almost always passed down from parents to children. The gender divide was not as prominent as it was in other countries. It was common for both sons and daughters to inherit land, wealth, and titles. Even in the paddy field, it was common for both men and women to work together, though some work, such as tilling the soil and ploughing, was almost always done by men (though I have seen a few rare exceptions as well.)

Preparing the soil before cultivation was something that was undertaken with great care, and also, great respect. Doing a roughshod job of it generally brought the wrath of the elders on the Juniors. They knew that plants would not grow to their fullest potential in infertile and badly-tilled soil. The harvest was what would either feed their families or would cause famine, and that was fundamentally decided by the soil and its preparation. As such, to neglect the duty of tilling the soil 'just right' was and is considered sacrilegious.

It must also be remembered that much of our agriculture is timed for the two monsoon seasons. So, there is that definitive window of time before the soil must be prepared. Too early, and there will not be enough rain to ensure the paddy grows; too late, and the soil is not ready and planting will have to happen in less-than-ideal soil, which the ancestors knew would adversely affect the harvest.

The heaviest 'labour' was generally during the Soil Preparation process. It was common for farmers to work 12-to-13-hour days during this period. It was also common for many in other professions to come and help, if required. Any 'idle' young man is also generally 'roped' in during this time, with meals provided to them (work was generally done free and the 'payment' was a meal – and if the harvest was exceptionally good, a small 'token' of paddy). This is because, if the field did not really have a good harvest, it was common for the entire village to not have their staple – rice.

Back in the day, when it was only what was not produced in the village that was brought into the village, and transactions in money were very limited, a bad harvest generally spelt disaster, and nearly six months of poverty and relative hunger.

It must be understood that 'poverty' in Sri Lanka is very different to other parts of the world, and especially India – its closest neighbour. Most of Sri Lanka is lush and 'green' and though harvests were affected, there was enough foraging that could be done. As such it was very rare for most Sri Lankans to ever hear of 'dying of hunger.' However, it was very much a fact that when crops failed, entire villages suffered. So, preparing the soil for the next season was considered a duty and a responsibility of the entire village, and it was very common for most to chip in.

Soil Preparation is critical in paddy cultivation. Similarly, ensuring the organisation is 'ready' is important to grow Leaders. Ensuring the 'soil' is ready for Leaders to be grown within an organisation requires three aspects to be considered: the 'mindset' of the organisation, ensuring the right frameworks are in place, and finally, ensuring that the resources are available.

Chapter 1

The Mindsets Required to Grow Leaders

"Most good things take time. Most instant things don't last. Unless you are willing to put in the time, Leaders will never grow..."

There is a certain mindset you need to be a farmer, and it is amazing that many of these mindsets are so, so vital if you want to 'grow' Leaders as well. Having the right 'mindset' is important and it is equally important to have this 'mindset' collectively shared as well. Unless it is collectively held, it becomes virtually impossible to truly work together and act when required.

Norms guide behaviours far more than we would like to recognise, and they certainly govern our behaviour a lot more than 'written laws.' Laws need a lot of effort to be enforced, but norms generally become 'inherent' behaviours by social pressures and related aspects, limiting and often completely taking away the need to 'enforce' things. Collective 'mindsets' or 'accepted norms' are what guided centuries of agricultural practices without the need to write anything down, nor having the need to 'enforce' behaviour.

Similarly, you need to have 'accepted norms' or 'mindsets' if an organisation is to truly grow Leaders. Without this collective conscience and set of firmly-held beliefs, developing Leaders becomes the sole charge of the HR Department, who are often asked to organise 'Leadership Development Programs' that identified Employees can attend.

So, before anything else, we need to understand the four key 'mindsets' that are needed as prerequisites for any form of attempt to grow Leaders of the future.

#1 Everyone has the potential to lead

Unless you believe that *everyone* has potential, you are going to be extremely narrow and limited in your talent pool selection. Sometimes, talent is not obvious. Sometimes, the best performers are under the radar and work silently, unbeknown to the Seniors. Sometimes, the best talent blossoms later. Sometimes, those who show promise, diminish in performance as pressures mount.

There are no definitives about people. Just like different plants have different timelines for their growth and blossoming, people are not all going to shine simply because you create an environment for this to happen. Also, remember that what is a conducive environment for one may not be so, for another. There are so many contextual considerations to make when it comes to people that you really cannot generalise anything.

So, you really need to *believe* in people and their potential. You need to truly have faith that everyone will rise to their potential eventually, and that everyone *has* this potential within them. It is a huge mistake to make comparisons.

Leadership is not a race to the finish line, nor is it a competition. Yet we make it into just that inside organisations. Leaders are Leaders, and they all can and will contribute their best towards a cause and a purpose – each in their own way.

If you approach people as people, rather than making comparisons, chances are you will get a lot more results from all of them, and what's more, you will have them collaborating instinctively rather than jostling for power and prestige.

Unless you start with this basic belief, you will never create environments and cultures where everyone can thrive. You will instead create a culture that becomes inhibitive and restrictive to many. You will also create a very unhealthy competition amongst people who should ideally work together.

#2 Not everyone will become a Leader, and that's okay

Sounds contradictory to the first belief? At first glance, yes; but, take a deeper look. Everyone has the potential, but not everyone wants to fulfil it, for whatever reason. Others want to but don't get there, for whatever reason. Potential and working on that potential until you fulfil it are two very different things. Everyone has the potential; only a few truly fulfil theirs.

You must be okay with the fact that not everyone you nurture and support will blossom into accomplished Leaders. Just because you water and take care of plants, notice that not all of them flourish in the same way and some, no matter what you do, may wither and die. That shouldn't stop you from watering the garden now, should it? Similarly, the fact that not everyone will truly make use of the opportunities you provide should not discourage you from investing in people. You must be okay with the odds playing out. It is quite normal for the law of averages to apply in Leadership development too.

We are not working with 'subordinates'. We are working with Leaders of the Future.

Want to grow Leaders? Then, you must stop looking at Employees as 'subordinates.' Rather, you must start looking at them as Leaders of the future. This simple mindset change makes a huge difference in how you approach people. Treat them like 'subordinates' and all you have is a bunch of paper pushers, and all you get is mere 'compliance.' Treat them like future Leaders, and you keep looking at how they can be groomed and you start creating opportunities for them to improve and grow. It also enables the entire organisation to drive the ethos that 'Juniors' need to be respected and valued, as they are the ones who will inherit the future organisation. This makes all the difference in the 'attitude' the entire organisation has toward 'Juniors' who will otherwise never be given opportunities simply because of tenure.

#3 Each individual is a person, and they have their own unique Leadership journey to undertake

Leadership truly is a journey one undertakes as much as life. Each individual will need to figure things out for themselves and it is rather ludicrous to expect them to learn from anything else apart from their own experience.

Unless organisations allow that space and time, Leadership development is looked upon in the same way as a mechanised conveyor belt, churning out Leaders of a certain mould. This is hugely counterproductive and also, extremely short-lived.

Unless you build wholesome, authentic and well-groomed Leaders, what you will have is a set of Leaders who will not be able to lead effectively when a crisis hits.

Allow each person to take their own journey. Stop the expectation of having a 'type' of Leader you want to create and also, resist the temptation to 'hurry' the process.

#4 Development of people is an investment into the future and we will make it irrespective of circumstance

Developing Leaders is costly. It takes time, energy and quite a substantial financial budget. Most of the time, organisations look at developing Leaders only when there are vacancies or structural gaps. This is too late. Leaders need to be groomed and readied as an ongoing process so that when the opportunities arise, they can seamlessly step in and take on the role. If you wait until there is a 'vacancy', chances are you will have individuals who take on higher levels of management who are ill-equipped to be Leaders.

The other common objection to developing Leaders and investing in the process is that these highly-trained and developed individuals will be headhunted by others. This can and often does happen. This is one of the reasons you should never simply train and develop a 'selected few.'

However, even if they are to leave the organisation at some point, the investment in Leaders will never really go to waste. It must be acknowledged, however, that as much as you invest in people, you must have mechanisms to safeguard that investment as well. As such, having solid retention frameworks becomes critical (which will be discussed later). 'They will leave' should never be an excuse not to make that investment in your future Leaders.

Growing Leaders is virtually impossible unless there is an overriding ethos and belief structure that acknowledges and pays homage to the importance of building people within the organisational setting. Unless organisations have this mindset, the growing of a Leader is simply limited to periodic 'Training Programs' that get done mostly as a reward and recognition attempt, rather than a development process. This collective mindset is critical if the organisation is to take a more organic and cyclical/ongoing approach to developing Leaders within their fold.

MAS Holdings is a business diversified conglomerate, with an annual revenue of US$ 2 billion. It is the largest Apparel and Apparel Tech company in South Asia, with a global footprint spanning across over fifteen countries. What started out as an 'experiment', thirty years ago, is currently Sri Lanka's largest private sector employer, with over 95,000 Employees being directly employed by the group, the majority of them based in Sri Lanka. The Founding Chairman, Deshamanya Mahesh Amalean, built MAS very much on the foundation of believing in people, their potential and the principle of "doing the right thing, because it was the right thing to do". He built factories that provide a comfortable and safe working space for people to thrive, personally and professionally, whilst being employed at MAS, which was a stark contrast to what the people in Sri Lanka were used to seeing – the 'sweatshops' for which the garment industry was known. Identifying the 'basics' of this ethical employment and working conditions was an important cornerstone which contributed to MAS' massive success.

He ensured that the work environments were plush and comfortable, he paid well above industry norms as salaries, and he gave his Teams complete autonomy to run the businesses without the general 'interference' common in family-run businesses. He also ensured he brought in 'talent' from various industries, making MAS a melting pot of skills, competencies, and potential.

Throughout the tenure and the thirty years, MAS has always stood on the firm belief that Employees are worthy of investment across the board. From the outset, Mahesh was clear that every single employee he had was someone who could and should be groomed to take on more as they go through their careers. This firm belief, from the very inception of the organisation, saw the proliferation of a culture that invested hugely in technical and soft skills development with a definitive focus on Leadership development. It soon became the 'University' that offered young new entrants the grooming they needed for their careers.

Many organisations soon started poaching MAS talent, but the founders and the Senior Management Teams held firm on their convictions and never cut back on their development initiatives. In fact, each year, they increased their budgets, and also, strengthened their HR frameworks even further to ensure MAS had a Leadership pipeline across the entire organisation. Many who started out as Sewing Operatives are Senior Managers today – something that would have been impossible in a traditional organisation at the time.

MAS's commitment to 'nurturing' and 'growing' well-rounded Leaders, through holistic efforts in people talent and people development. These include some of the most steadfast policy-level affirmations to development, including never having any form of financial bond to be signed for the development Employees receive.

Some have benefitted from training and development in institutions such as The Harvard Business School, Stanford, and The Center for Creative Leadership. They also offer full scholarships to do MBAs as well as technical qualifications. No bonding agreements are required for any of these scholarships.

Many have taken the benefits and left the organisation soon afterwards. Still, over the years, MAS has never slowed down their development initiatives, nor signed any bond to retain Employees after being developed. Mahesh's immortal words have always been: "We develop people because we want them to reach their fullest potential. Whether they stay with us or not, if the training we offer enables them to be the best versions of themselves, then, we have achieved our objective."

Chapter 2

Essential Frameworks that enable Leaders

"Leaders are not born. They are not 'made' in a vacuum either. If you want Leaders to be 'grown' you need to build the right ecosystem first..."

HR Frameworks play a big part in creating a learning culture that is essential if Leaders are to be grown within the organisation. Frameworks need to be interlinked and interconnected if they are truly to make an impact, and the organisation needs to be looking at each part of the employee lifecycle.

Two fundamental frameworks that must exist to ensure there is uniformity and structure around the development of Leaders are the Values Framework and the Leadership Competency Framework. Needless to say, there needs to be proper thought invested in creating both, rather than simply picking generic values and competencies from a 'list' of available 'words.'

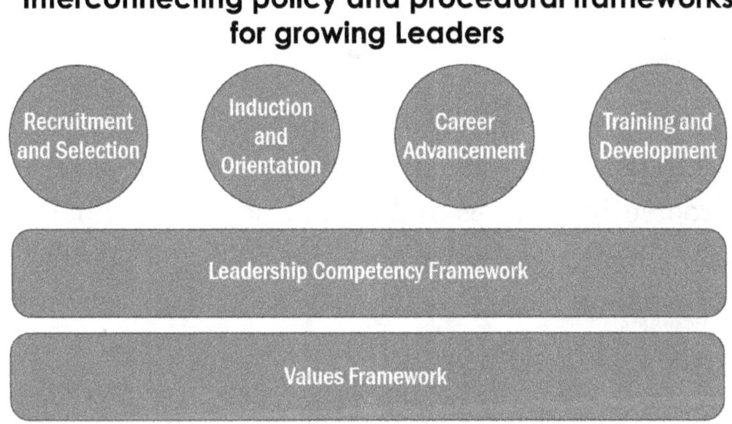

Most organisations look at Values from a moralistic perspective. Values need to be contingent on, and reflective of where the organisation wants to be, rather than simply what they believe in as 'good behaviours.' Similarly, Leadership Competencies must be pegged to what kind of behaviours Leaders are required to have to drive the business towards its Vision and Mission.

Unless there is alignment in these asspects, the kind of Leaders the organisation develops may not actually be the type of Leaders who can bring in the results the organisation is envisaging.

It is important to undertake building both these frameworks as an exercise that works with, and takes into consideration, three critical elements:

- The Vision and the Mission and the Key Objectives of the organisation
- The type of industry the organisation is part of, and its 'contextual' realities
- The aspirations of the people in it

Values and Competency Frameworks must not be undertaken purely as an 'academic' exercise and must be rooted in realities and expectations. It is important to involve the entire organisation in it, rather than its maintenance merely being the domain of the Senior Management Team.

Ensuring that the wider organisation is involved in the development of these frameworks also helps in ensuring there is a wider buy-in from the key employee stakeholders, and also, ensures that it becomes a 'living' document rather than simply something that is there for ornamental purposes.

One of the best examples of Values being built using a bottom-up approach was seen in 2008 when Mobitel undertook the creation of its Vision, Mission, and Values. The then CEO, Suren, had taken over what was a telecom company that was in the doldrums, and given it a new lease of life.

When Suren took over, the company was suffering from poor performance and was very much in the red. With clear strategy and amazing insight, Suren focused on some superlative branding work that saw Mobitel become the forerunner in the prepaid space and become a true contender to take on the market Leader Dialog.

In order to galvanise the organisation, which was partly owned by the state (and the 'red tape' that came with it) Suren thought it was important to have a new Vision, Mission and very importantly, Values. Rather than simply having a workshop which involved the Senior Team, Suren wanted the entire organisation involved in the process, and in offering input.

His brief to us was quite clear: 'I want a Vision, Mission and Values that EVERYONE relates to and thinks of as THEIR OWN.' I still remember the twinkle in his eye when he said 'I want everyone reading our Vision, Mission and Values to feel that THEY authored it.'

So began a three-month-long process which saw over 50 focus groups being created, covering over 800 Employees from minor staff all the way to the Senior Management and even the Chairperson. The aspirations and insights were collated and common threads identified.

Amazingly there was a huge level of congruence that was absolutely evident to see. So, when the final brainstorming work-shops took place, the Vision, Mission and Values were crafted seamlessly. Case in point, 7 out of the 8 values identified were common across 80% of the total sample population who took part in the FGDs.

When Suren launched the new Vision, Mission and Values to the entire population over a gala dinner, he got that ever-elusive standing ovation. In the truest testimony to its relevance, the Values were revisited five times over in the last decade and more, and every time, the organisation felt that the Values they came up with in 2008 were still valid, and should not be changed. They felt they stood for all that Mobitel should and must stand for and to this date, they stand, with just a few minor adjustments (mostly because many felt NOT changing it at least a little might send the wrong message as being 'complacent!')

Competency Frameworks play a huge role in articulating what type of behaviour Leaders at different levels of the organisation must demonstrate. Ultimately, unless you *know* what is expected of you as a Leader, organisations tend to leave Leadership to being something subjective and individualistic. Though individuality and authenticity are critical in Leadership, it is also important to ensure there is a common set of behaviours *everyone* commits to, which is what develops a culture that is congruent and integrated.

As such, Leadership Competency Frameworks need to be framed with a clear understanding of what type of Leaders are best suited for the organisation at that moment in time.

Another key consideration is to ensure that Competency Frameworks are interconnected and complementary. Each level of Leadership needs to be something that helps the other levels and should not be simply about 'ideal' behaviours. Leadership Competency Frameworks are best when both 'leading' and 'following' are intertwined.

Once the Values and Competency Frameworks are in place, it is important to link them to the key HR frameworks: that of Recruitment, Induction and Orientation, Career Advancement and Training and Development. Unless the Competencies and Values are integrated into the HR frameworks they never quite become 'living' frameworks – and simply become 'documents.'

- At recruitment, use the values and competencies to craft questions to probe thinking. Use it for the references being sought. Weave them into assessment centre-type selection processes.
- At induction and orientation, build in a module around Values and Competencies. Ensure each level understands *why* these frameworks are important and *why* they need to live by them. Explain, at orientation itself, how Competencies and Values will become a key criterion for advancement within the organisation.
- Career Advancement: ensure Values and Competencies are assessed through instruments such as 360s, Development Centres/Assessment Centres, formal and informal feedback loops and even observations, and incorporate this into being 'quantifiable' data to populate the 9 box type frameworks.

- Training and Development: All Leadership development initiatives need to ultimately be pegged to values, and competencies. Unless *all* development work is aligned, all they become is simply 'Programs' with no real linkage to anything tangible.

Hirdaramani Group is a 100-plus-year organisation that pioneered the apparel industry in Sri Lanka. Hirdaramani is a great example of the adoption of a set of solid conceptual frameworks that became the backbone of Leadership development within the organisation.

As with most organisations that grow organically, Hirdaramani's frameworks grew over time; but something they did brilliantly well was taking stock of the different 'elements' which had evolved, and interlinking them, to ensure there is a clear connection between each one.

Here are some elements from their key policy and procedural frameworks:

A. *The Senior Management Team has a Leadership Code that is the 'bible' they must live by. This Code is something that each senior Leader gets peer-reviewed on periodically, and 360s conducted for formal appraisal processes.*

B. *The induction and orientation Program has an entire module on Values and Competencies where new recruits are informed of not only how important Values are but also warned in no uncertain terms that Values are NOT NEGOTIABLE.*

They are also informed about how they can bring any grievance to the HR Team in confidence and that if they ever see any of their superiors breaking values, they MUST report it IMMEDIATELY.

C. *A Leadership competency framework has been developed to look at Leadership-specific competencies at supervisory (non-executive category) levels, as well as Executive, Assistant Manager, Manager and General Manager categories within the hierarchy. Each competency is linked to the others, ensuring that each group has a direct impact through their behaviour on the other.*

D. *The Competency Framework is the 'base' for all the 360 Reviews done as part of the Development and Career Advancement initiatives. Career Advancement is curtailed unless values are lived, and competencies developed.*

E. *There are Leadership-specific Development Programs built for each tier of the hierarchy, starting from a Supervisory Development Program, Leadership Development Program, Advanced Leadership Program as well as an Accelerator Program (for top talent). Each Program is designed based on the Competency Framework, and has assessments at the end to track Competency Development as well as the application of learning. Each Program is also designed to act as part of 'linked' Programs – so that whatever you learn in one is augmented at the next level Program.*

F. *ALL career advancement also factors in the successful completion of the different Leadership Programs done at each level. They not only have to complete the Program, but also the Projects which Participants are given. Those who have not committed to their development are not given advancement within the organisation.*

Having these frameworks in place have enabled the organisation not only to grow Leaders but also, to ensure there is a certain homogeneity in the type of Leaders groomed. This has enabled the easy transition of Leaders from one manufacturing plant to another – not only within Sri Lanka but also to other global locations, in which the organisation has facilities.

This ability to move across the organisation seamlessly has helped tremendously in being able to grow and retain top talent in a fiercely competitive industry. What is very clear is that the frameworks become the foundation for the development of Leaders across the hierarchy. It has also enabled a certain transparency that has given credibility to the advancement process overall, establishing the importance of values-led Leaders across the board.

Chapter 3

Resource Allocations to Grow Leaders

"If you give time, if you give attention and focus, if you work on it daily, and if you have faith, almost anything can be grown – almost anywhere. Leaders are no different..."

Whenever resources are discussed with regard to Leadership development, it almost always becomes a conversation about money. However, what has been made abundantly clear when it comes to growing Leaders is that time is a far more important consideration than a financial budget. This is not to say that carving out a budget for training and development is not important – it certainly is – but it is far, far more important that organisations take the *time* to really grow Leaders. So, let's discuss time as a resource first.

Leaders are best taught by other Leaders. Most Managers are pressed for time and many consider that grooming those under them is an 'additional task' that often becomes a 'by the way' activity. Organisations that take growing Leaders seriously understand and live by the fact that developing Leaders is an integral part of a Manager's job, and that Leaders ought to grow more Leaders – not simply expect compliance and halfhearted followers.

Growing Leaders require organisations to embrace the importance of spending time with 'Juniors', not only in chit chat and fellowship but in serious conversations around Leadership, and carving time to mentor and groom them on an ongoing basis.

A farmer, no matter how rich they may be, still needs to put in the 'time' to grow crops. There is no substitute for putting time in. In fact, investing time is the absolute yardstick of how 'serious' you are as a farmer.

A good farmer does not consider growing crops a pain, or a 'job', or a 'task', or a 'KPI'... they consider it the core of their being. Farming is not a vocation or a livelihood per se, it is a way of life.

Growing Leaders is the same. If you are serious about having a solid Leadership pipeline, forget the money for a moment and ask yourself how much *time* are you willing to commit to it. What on earth do you want *that* much time for?

- Time for deep observations, and making notes so that you can discuss your observations with them.
- Time to think about what area each individual needs to grow in, and how this can be brought about. Time to make plans for them.
- Time for wide-open conversations and dialogue about behaviours, results, and everything in between. Time to really discuss, rather than pass comments. Time to really listen as much as talk.
- Time to get both formal and informal feedback about those in your charge, and time to collate that feedback to make coherent, constructive, and impactful conversation material.
- Time to reflect on what you can do to support and grow those under and around you. Time to reflect on how you can best give them the leg up they need.
- Time to design Projects that will enable those you are growing to showcase their talent. Time to find opportunities for them to really put their talent to good use.

Most of the time, *time* is what is never given to young Leaders. Most 'bosses' are too 'busy' with their day-to-day work, and are blindsided by the fact that their primary objective is to grow those who are with them. Most superiors forget that growing Leaders across the organisation should and must be one of their primary charges.

Time is an investment the organisation must be willing to make if they want Leaders to grow. Time not only from the 'Seniors' but also time from the 'Juniors.'

- Time for young Leaders to step outside their routine chores and engage in something more strategic.
- Time for them to go for seminars, workshops, and training Programs, without being made to feel 'guilty' for taking that time off, or worse still, demanding they stay back without going for the Program because of 'urgent' work.
- Time for the youngsters to invest their energy towards innovative solutions and suggestions.
- Time for them to 'think' and 'reflect.'
- Time to just 'wander about' the premises, make friends, and have chit-chats.

Leaders are not grown in 9-5 timetables. Leaders are not grown in sterile environments either. Leaders need the space and the opportunity to grow. All of which have time as a prerequisite. Many forget that time is the biggest inhibiting factor for the growth of Leaders, though many organisations never do this intentionally.

Though there are well-documented best practices from organisations such as 3M and Google that make it a company policy to give their Employees 'time' to work on Projects that they are passionate about, the conscious, formal allocation of time to 'grow Leaders' is not common.

Many think of 'time' allocation purely as a 'formal' exercise when it should not be the case. The 'allocated' and often 'measured' time (as a KPI in the form of 'hours' dedicated for 'training') is often merely a box-ticking exercise.

What is more important is a general ethos that young Leaders need to be mentored and coached on an ongoing basis, and that the 'Seniors' need to be 'willing' to give that time. If this becomes a 'norm', it happens without ever having to formalise the process.

As much as it *is* important to ensure there are formal time allocations for Coaching, Training and Mentoring initiatives, it is equally (or dare I say *more*) important to ensure that there is a culture of growing Leaders that enables everyone to carve out time for this purpose.

A wonderful example of growing Leaders within the organisation, and ensuring there is focused time for this was seen at the former CARE offices in Sri Lanka.

Given that NGOs work on 'contracts' rather than full-time employment, it is quite common for many to have their contracts end once the Project comes to an end, making them redundant in the process. Though it was common for many of them to be reinstated in different Projects, it was also quite common for many to be made 'jobless' at the end of their tenure.

CARE Sri Lanka identified this as an 'issue' very early on, and devoted concerted time to build, not only technical expertise but broader skills, that would enable the Employees to find alternative employment in other NGOs or corporates after their Projects come to a close.

Though never formally institutionalised in a process per se, the organisation had a 'culture' of devoting considerable time towards building soft skills, offering wider exposure, having frequent 'touch bases', the ability to move laterally within the organisation and dabble in different Projects, all of which enabled Employees across the organisation to hone their Leadership skills.

The 'informal' process was so good that almost anyone who worked with CARE was able to find alternative employment once their Projects ended, as they were known to be a 'cut above anyone else' within the sector.

CARE Sri Lanka was often looked at as the 'university' for the sector. The growth did NOT happen because of formal training or structured training per se but through a series of job enlargements, wider exposure, focused time in conversations with Seniors about their strengths and weaknesses, as well as many opportunities to 'get involved' in many strategic initiatives. Case in point, CARE's LRSP (Long Range Strategic Planning) process involved EVERYONE within the fold – including drivers and minor staff. They not only offered their input; they were also involved in the final workshop where they decided on the future direction of the organisation. This inclusive exposure enabled everyone across the organisation to partake in the decision-making and strategic processes – and enabled the building of Leadership skills from a very early stage in their careers. This 'time' away from their 'routine' work is something many attribute as the number one reason why they believe they 'grew' as Leaders whilst at CARE Sri Lanka.

Another important resource, of course, is the financials. Though a 'training budget' per se is not the only pre-requisite, it is a good starting point. Many organisations pay lip service to grooming Leaders but fail to really put their money where their mouth is.

Many fail to really have a solid budget to enable people development and far too often, the training budget is the *first* budget to be taken out when there is any sign of 'trouble' in the 'external environment.' A definitive budget is important to ensure people can be grown into their fullest potential as Leaders.

However, *what* this money is spent for is more important than having the budget itself. Many organisations that do carve out budgets never really understand how to maximise this budget, and famously monitor 'training hours per employee' as their yardstick of how well the money was spent.

Measuring 'man hours' is never a good enough measurement to assess the effectiveness of development initiatives, nor is the $ spent per person. Development initiatives must be measured by the impact they make and the competencies grown (which we will discuss at length later). As such, ensuring there is a budget, and the ability to measure ROI after training is, ultimately, the only sustainable way to ensure training spent becomes an investment. The inability to do so makes it just a 'cost', which is why it is always at knife's edge when it comes to cost-cutting initiatives.

Having a definitive budget to grow Leaders demonstrates a commitment to Leadership development. It also ensures that developing Leaders do not become a 'nice to have' but rather an integral and important part of the overall organisation's ethos and fundamental belief system. This also ensures that Employees within the organisation take heart in understanding that their organisation is committed to their growth and development, irrespective of the challenges the organisation faces.

Both MAS and Hirdaramani Groups have stood steadfast in their conviction that training budgets should be the last to be curtailed in times of crisis. Even during Covid, both organisations carried forward with their development initiatives. Sure, there were cutbacks, but even with relatively lower budgets, the development initiatives were planned out for the year, in ways which could be effectively carried out despite restrictions in travel/movement and medical safety, and which still took place.

Case in point, the Hirdaramani Group carried out their Leadership Development Program for Emerging Leaders even during the lockdown. Even though it was clear that some may even be downsized, the training for these individuals was not cut back. Switching to online mode, the company carried forward their signature Leadership Development Program, and ensured they carried through with Projects after training as planned – demonstrating a three times the investment in cost-saving initiatives the Participants collectively completed. This saving was reinvested in training budgets, ensuring that the company carried forward development initiatives across the board, including sessions for Sewing Operatives, in order for them to build resilience and confidence in what was one of the (if not THE) most difficult periods in their organisation's history.

Many claim that the confidence they gained during this tumultuous time has stood them in good stead in their roles and career advancement.

The other, often forgotten 'resource' that organisations need to have at their disposal if they are committed to grow Leaders is proper role models and 'heroes.' Far too often organisations celebrate the wrong 'type' of 'Leader', born out of misunderstanding 'charisma' and 'results'

to mean Leadership. Remember, we mimic who we idolise, and this is possibly the fastest way of assimilating behaviours.

Just as a young child will mimic their parents, young aspirants inside an organisation mimic their 'Leaders', especially Leaders who are 'celebrated' by the organisation. Have the wrong role models, and chances are that you are perpetuating the growth of the wrong type of Leader within the organisation.

Having great Leaders is not enough; the organisation needs to make sure that they are 'celebrated', otherwise, popular culture sets in, and the 'wrong type' becomes the 'icon' that gets all the 'glory.' More often than not, great Leaders are not about the 'show' – rather, they are about 'substance.'

Most great Leaders do a poor job of 'marketing' themselves. So, being able to identify and showcase great Leadership within the organisation needs to be an integral part of the Senior Management and HR Domains. Nothing will grow poor Leaders faster than showcasing and celebrating the 'wrong' type of Leader.

Remember, you propagate what you celebrate. Period.

If you choose to 'celebrate' a particular 'type' of Leader, you must be okay with the fact that the Leadership that is grown within the organisation will be just that, and that expecting something different is absolutely naïve. No matter what policies or procedures you have, the behaviour you grow in your young Leaders is the same as that which you choose to celebrate.

Slimline, under Dian Gomes, and Hirdaramani Woven, under Tony Nadaraja, could not have been more different, though both organisations were extremely successful in their own right.

Dian was the out-and-out maverick known for his flamboyancy and superlative branding of his organisation and himself.

Tony on the other hand was hardly known outside of his organisation, and was, for all intents and purposes, very much the 'low-key' CEO. Tony rose from the ranks, with no formal education apart from the 13th grade, working himself up from being a casual, weekly-paid supervisor all the way to being the CEO.

Dian was a CIMA-qualified accountant working for KPMG when he was headhunted to MAS, being a Financial Controller before he was given the mantle of MD of the Slimline division of MAS Intimates. Dian made Slimline the envy of the entire industry, having the first Gym, the first Boxing Ring, five-star accommodation, off-the-chart salaries, and also, absolutely wild parties that soon became the stuff of legend. Tony, on the other hand, was very much about technical expertise, focused attention on basics, hard work, and almost zero 'flash.' Dian's Slimline recruited graduates from Harvard and Stanford, as well as the best of the best graduates from all over the island, most of whom spoke with strong American or British accents. Tony's Woven had mostly Sinhala-speaking individuals – even at Senior Management levels - and showcased raw talent who could not afford to go to campus locally (let alone overseas.).

Today, both have retired. Both left their organisations as top-class entities often showcased as 'benchmarks' in their own right. Both organisations have continued to grow and prosper after they left, but the type of Leaders that they have propagated have been vastly different.

The cultures of Leadership they both left behind are almost polar opposite and continue to be distinctly differentiated. What is interesting to see is that many of the Leaders Dian and Tony groomed under them have left their respective organisations (some have even left the industry). However, the 'style' of Leadership their 'proteges' adopt is very similar to their own.

This is a rather classic example of having 'role models' that others mimic, and the kind of Leaders' organisations propagate by simply 'following' the Leaders' behaviour.

Time, Financials and Role Models are three key resources organisations need to put in place in order to grow Leaders within the organisational fold. Unless all three are in place, Leaders who are developed might not be fully formed.

Without budgets, young Leaders may not have the exposure to different ideas, thoughts, views, and practices which are possible only with outside interventions.

Without the time, (and without being trained directly by others, and not only by Leadership Programs), young Leaders will lack the opportunities to really practise Leadership, and also, might not really be 'free' to make mistakes and learn from them.

Without proper role models, Leaders may be culturally insensitive, or worse still, mimic the wrong behaviours to the detriment of themselves and their organisation.

To grow wholesome Leaders, all three resources must be present.

Part 2

Planting

Once the soil is prepared, the farmers move into the planting phase. Until very recently, this was done purely manually. Here, both the farmer and their wives generally get involved, as do the children if they are of a certain age.

The planting process has a certain 'tacit knowledge' required. The 'seeds' are 'thrown' into the prepared soil in a certain rhythmic manner, which, unless this is done just right, is hugely wasteful or sub-optimal. Today, there are a few simple innovations that have enabled farmers to 'plant' in straight lines with geometric precision without wasting the precious seeds. However, back then, and even today in certain places, it was and is done manually, as it was done through the centuries.

Possibly the toughest part of this phase is not the planting per se, but making sure the weeds in the paddy field are taken out. Today, most farmers resort to weedicides to get rid of the trouble, but back then, it was done by back-breaking manual work. Some, including some of my uncles, still do it this way.

Almost all weedicides cause a lot of environmental damage and therefore, some farmers still prefer to stick to the 'old ways.' Weeding generally involves going row by row, painstakingly picking the weeds, which takes a ton of time and a bigger portion of the effort. If you miss one, then, it generally spells disaster as it takes over the field. So, weeding is something that both the farmers and their entire families get involved in, and is taken absolutely seriously as an undertaking.

Another important facet of the planting process is that the farmers carve out the 'best seeds' of rice for planting, not for consumption. When the harvesting happens, there are three major 'grades' of grain into which the rice crop gets segregated. The best grade is for replanting. The second is for consumption or sale. The other is threshed and used for animal feed, or sometimes to make flour out of (this is not the case today) where the best gets used for flour mills.

Back in the day, flour was made manually and the fact that the grain was damaged and not of the same 'weight' did not really matter and as such, it was the lowest 'grades' that were used for making flour. So, it is the *best* of the *best* that is chosen for replanting. Why? Because they are the ones that have the potential to have the highest yields.

As much as planting, making sure the Leaders are 'planted' is important within an organisational setting. Not everyone will be a Leader, nor does everyone want to be a Leader. There is a certain element of 'luck' in who will make it and who will not, but you cannot really leave it all in the hands of 'Lady Luck'. The organisation needs to ensure that the odds are in the favour of the Leaders you plan to grow within it.

As much as you select seeds for planting, ensuring you select the right Leaders to grow becomes important. As much as you carefully weed the field, making sure you induct the right Leaders, and removing the wrong ones also becomes important. As much as you look after the young plants, supporting the growth of the fledgling Leaders becomes important.

Chapter 4

Identifying Leaders and Spotting Talent

"Bad seeds give bad yields – it's that simple."

Whenever you invest time and energy to plant, it is with the expectation of a yield. Leaders are no different. If you are investing time, energy, resources, and expertise into growing Leaders, you need to ensure there is a yield out of it, and the yield is simple; creating wholesome Leaders who will enable the organisation to grow and prosper.

As much as ancestral farmers ensured the best seeds were kept for planting, the best talent must be identified to be 'invested' in. Unless you identify the right talent, chances are you will be investing in the wrong talent pool. However, it is important at the outset to consider the fact that people are *not* static entities, and that they evolve all the time. As such, you need to closely watch the entire population and identify who is showing promise and when, so that your development processes can kick in. What is important to accept, though, are two very simple realities:

A. First, the organisation does not have unlimited resources (time or money) to be able to invest in everyone within the organisation. Some form of selection needs to happen at some point
B. Second, just because you spot talent and start growing these individuals does not guarantee that you will get them to truly blossom as Leaders. As such, you need to have pipelines built all the time.

Generally, the process of identifying talent and Leadership potential is pegged to the performance appraisal process. Here, possibly the most commonly used tool is the 9 Box, where performance and potential are mapped and the key talent is identified. This is a good process to follow. However, two major considerations need to be in place:

- Both performance and potential need to be measured using data. Performance must not be based on 'subjective' elements and potential must not be based on one person's opinion. Ensuring you have data (accurate and verified) is critical to ensure that the right people are identified. Otherwise, the 9 Box becomes merely an 'opinion' of a few, or worse still, simply an afterthought after individuals have been already identified and decided upon.

9 Box Grid[1]

- It is important that the data feeds are cumulative rather than event-based, especially for potential. Having ongoing feedback being collated is important rather than a one-off 360 or feedback through a career committee which can have many biases.

1 The 9-box model was first introduced by McKinsey & Company in the 1970s. It was initially developed as a framework to help General Electric (GE) prioritize investments across different business units. It later evolved into a talent management tool, plotting employees based on their current performance and future potential. While the exact origin and creator of the 9-box model are not well-documented, McKinsey is credited with popularising it through their work with GE. It has since become a widely used tool in talent management and succession planning.

Identifying Leaders becomes important to ensure you are able to really hone in on those on whom you will focus your time and energies, for development initiatives.

One of the best ways to identify potential Leaders is to ask for Volunteers for special Projects. Many shy away from taking on more responsibility, and few will volunteer for Projects whilst being engaged in a demanding job. So, make a habit of seeking Volunteers and see who will raise their hands. Give opportunities for young Leaders to showcase their potential by creating opportunities for them.

The HAY Project was something that MAS undertook to develop a core set of competencies[1] *as well as look at how best to structure their growing business units in a systematic and structured way.*

The first Project was a groundbreaking Project for Sri Lanka. It was the first time a Pay and Grading initiative was undertaken by any organisation on the island. It was also the first time a best-of-class HR Consulting organisation did a major Project in Sri Lanka.

The HAY Project was one of the key initiatives MAS undertook towards developing a world-class HR practice within the business. Though there were identified individuals for the Project, MAS opened up the opportunity for Volunteers so that those within the

1 The Hay Group was a global management consulting firm specialising in areas like leadership development, talent management, and organisational effectiveness. In 2015, Hay Group was acquired by Korn Ferry, another major player in the consulting industry.

different plants could train and develop themselves on the HAY methodology.

Some of the Volunteers stepped into the Project though they were senior professionals within the fold already, and were uncertain where they would 'end up' after the Project. However, they volunteered because they wanted to grow, and those who did were later able to leapfrog in their careers, given that they acquired technical expertise in pay, grading, job descriptions, job evaluations, and Competency Frameworks, which became cornerstones of the organisational structures which developed as the business grew further.

The volunteering also enabled the HR organisation within the company to identify young potential Leaders for the future, many of whom helm the HR function within the clusters of MAS, today.

Another way of identifying talent is to offer Projects outside of their individual domain expertise to manage and lead. Leadership is really tested when you are without titles and 'power', and Projects that are outside of the domain expertise are excellent opportunities for this.

As part of the Leadership Development Program run for Hirdaramani for entry-level Leadership roles, there is a Project that each Participant must complete that is outside of their JD and KPIs. The Project is two months in duration and has a definitive process to follow, including a Project Proposal Phase, an Execution Phase, and a Reporting Stage, as well as a Presentation to the Senior

Team on the outcomes and learning. This is used as an opportunity to look at young talent and see if they can be better utilised in different areas, expanding their scope whilst developing 'General Managers' of the future.

One example of an individual who truly made use of this opportunity was Udana Warnakulasooriya who was a Merchandiser at the time of doing the Program. Udana's Project was something that no one really expected, and his ability to put his learning into practice in something that was not his domain, and bring a definitive result enabled the organisation to identify his potential. He was given an opportunity to move into Operational Excellence and Lean, and he took the brave step to move not only his area/expertise but also, boldly moved to Vietnam to take on the new role.

His exposure to lean practices, and to implementing lean practices in manufacturing as well as merchandising, truly broadened his horizons. Udana developed and honed his skills so well that he was able to move industries completely, and is today the COO of JAGRO – which grows strawberries and other high end produce for the Indian, Maldivian and Middle Eastern markets, and operates greenfield to commercial operations in Rwanda, Africa, one of the first agricultural companies out of Sri Lanka to do this.

There are often 'wild cards,' those who are often not quite 'picked up' by formal processes. It is important to look a little beyond the 9 Box and other formal processes to see if there are 'hidden gems' of talent in the organisation.

A good way to spot such talent is to *ask* – especially skip levels and ask about who they find has Leadership potential. Customers and other stakeholders can also be good sources of insights.

An interesting method of choosing Leaders is practised at Methodist College Colombo. A 100+ year girls school established by the Methodist Missionaries, Methodist College has a selection process for their 'House Vice Captains' and 'Prefects.'

Rather than Teachers and the Principal selecting positions, at Methodist, the Teachers only nominate the candidates based on applications put in.

The final decision of who takes on the position is left to be determined by a vote involving all the Senior Girls of the school. Often, those who are considered the most 'obvious' choices are not selected by the student community, where the relationships they have had come to the fore for selection of the Leaders for each house.

It is also important to understand that Leadership potential needs to be brought in anew to organisations as well. As much as promoting from within, it is important to infuse new blood into the organisation. This is often tricky, as many struggle to really fit into new cultures and Leadership positions that are filled from outside are often a hit-or-miss kind of gamble. As such, the recruitment of new Leaders to the organisation needs to be considered carefully – especially if the 'right' kind of Leader is to be brought in.

Brandix – another Garment Industry Giant in Sri Lanka – has put in place a scheme to encourage Employees to 'nominate' their friends for positions inside the organisation. In doing so, Employees take full responsibility for their referrals, ensuring that the candidates they recommended are well vetted and highly suitable for the role.

This approach has proven to be extremely successful – at almost all levels of the business. Many senior positions are not even advertised, and are sourced solely through 'known contacts.' Many in the company are also favourably considered for positions within the wider group that involves Pheonix Plastics, DTM Buttons, Hangers and American & Efird Thread. Many within the core Brandix organisation are placed in these sister companies for more senior Leadership positions, and are brought back with wider industry exposure and expertise.

Identifying Leadership Potential is important. Whether within the organisation or from outside, Leaders need to be identified and groomed. If the wrong selection is made, the investment you make will obviously not yield the results you wish. As such, ensuring there are robust systems and processes in place to identify not only the 'obvious' choices, but also those 'not so obvious' choices, becomes important.

Chapter 5

Inducting Leaders

"Simply giving a man a plough
is not enough
to make him a farmer..."

Leaders need to be inducted into the organisation as well as their roles. Induction and orientation are critical if you want Leaders to truly bind with the organisation ethos and culture, as well as contribute positively towards the overall objectives of the organisation.

One of *the* most important elements of an induction process for Leadership positions is one with the purpose of the organisation that truly buys into its Vision and Mission.

One of my colleagues was a former Major in the Sri Lankan Army. He overlooked the logistics during the final push for Sri Lanka's liberation war from the LTTE[1]*. One of the deep insights he offered was the difference in how the LTTE cadres were inducted into their organisation as opposed to how the Army inducted soldiers.*

The Army focused a lot on training, and they assumed that the new recruits were committed to the cause. The LTTE, on the other hand, developed an induction Program that was aimed at 'brainwashing' any member joining their ranks, and ensuring that they were firmly committed to the cause. They understood that belief in the cause was possibly more important than the individual's competency as a soldier; and this commitment, absolute obedience and die-hard fanaticism is what made all the difference.

Irrespective of whether you were an LTTE sympathiser or not, one must admire the ability of a mere 5,000-10,000 cadres being able to hold the fort against over 200,000 combined cadres of the Army, Navy and Air Force of Sri Lanka. In their heyday, the LTTE laid claim to nearly 30%-40% of the total land mass of the island.

1 The Liberation Tigers of Tamil Eelam, a militant separatist group fighting for an independent homeland for Hindu Tamils in northeastern Sri Lanka. Whether this was a war to regain the sovereignty of the nation is not debated. How it was carried out is often a bone of contention.

Disclaimer: The practices of the Liberation Tigers of Tamil Eelam (LTTE) are referenced in this book as an illustrative example. This reference does not imply any affinity, affiliation, commendation, or partisanship towards any party involved in the Sri Lankan civil war. This work does not endorse war or violence and acknowledges the profound loss and destruction that war inflicts upon a nation and its people.

The LTTE inducted Leaders with true zeal. Their orientation Programs included showing hours upon hours upon hours of video footage of atrocities that were done to the Tamils during the '83 riots, often referred to as 'Black July'.

After each video, the LTTE trainers would talk at length about the absolute 'cannibals' the Sinhalese were, and work the young cadres into a frenzy about the need for retribution. Some of these 'orientation' sessions lasted several months, and the more 'potential' they thought the young cadres had, the more focused was the orientation.

One of the key features of the LTTE orientation Program was that there were several different variations of the Program, depending on who was getting inducted. If they were simply 'foot soldiers' who were merely to 'shoot', then far less of an orientation took place. However, the more 'strategic' the cadre was, the more intense the orientation became.

Loyalty to the cause was considered of paramount importance. Compared to a typical soldier who joins the army, the 'orientation' was common to all. Depending on rank of course, but, irrespective of 'rank' the typical 'orientation' was far more focused on skill development than an 'indoctrination.'

The LTTE's 'orientation' framework was built on some key principles which are important when growing Leaders (as opposed to 'Employees')

- The loyalty to the cause is far more important than loyalty to a person. The LTTE placed a huge focus on the cause, and though there certainly was an undisputed Leader who would not be challenged at any point (Prabhakaran was, for all intentions and purposes, a ruthless dictator), the cause was 'beyond' the Leader as well. The orientation, first and foremost, was about the cause.
- There was a clear focus on values. Absolute loyalty to the cause and the Leader, willingness to sacrifice anything (including your life, your family and all your belongings) towards the cause, complete obedience, unwavering resolve, tenacity and cunning bravery. These were some of the core values instilled through the training during the orientation process.
- Orientation was not a one-off process, it was an ongoing process. Especially for those identified for Leadership positions, there were recurring 'sessions' that reaffirmed the importance of the cause and 'absolute hatred towards the Sinhalese' were reiterated at every opportunity.
- Orientation was not simply done by 'Seniors', it was done by peers, Seniors as well as others, including families who were adversely affected by the atrocities of the '83 riots. This made the induction more 'compelling'
- As part of the orientation, the cadres were 'tested' for their 'loyalty.' This, for many who were identified

for more strategic roles, often included 'executing' a family member or close friend for 'betraying the cause.'

Though gruesome and cringeworthy in every aspect, the LTTE's 'induction' of a 'Leader' offers some instructive lessons to consider when it comes to inducting Leaders within organisations.

Like the LTTE, you need to induct Leaders into a 'cause' as much as the organisation. We generally limit induction to 'Employees', and don't really have a different orientation for those we identify as 'Leaders.' Making this distinction, and ensuring we are able to truly bind those we identify towards Leadership positions to further the organisation's ethos, purpose and vision or 'cause' is critically important if Leaders are to lead with passion and zeal. It is not enough for Leaders to 'like' or 'love' the organisation, they must become, in LTTE terms, committed proponents of the mission.

A great illustration of an 'induction' that bordered on near fanatical fervor and zeal towards the cause, was seen when Slimline (one of the plants within the MAS umbrella – and possibly one of its most celebrated, even to date) took on a group of individuals to become the first company to implement SAP[2] *AFS (Apparel and Footwear Solution) in Sri Lanka. The advertisement that ran was famously titled the 'astronauts' advertisement and was an iconoclastic advert in every sense. It also attracted a*

2 Systems Applications and Products.

huge response – even though no one really knew what SAP was, at the time!

The recruitment process was arduous and gruelling, and those selected were given a huge pride of place within the organisation. They had their own 'command centre' as well as brand new laptops (a luxury at the time when only Senior Managers had a laptop) along with free rein over their Project. Working with SAP consultants, the Team was constantly 'inducted' into the ethos of the 'mission' which was to ensure they become a showcase for the rest of the organisation and work to make certain that SAP went 'live' on the due date. Over and again, the Teams were made to believe they were special, that they were destined to become legends, and also, that this 'mission' came first before anything else.

The core Team that implemented the first SAP rollout bonded so well that many still keep in touch with each other, even when many have left the organisation. Most, even after a decade or more of leaving the organisation will possibly look at Slimline as their 'true home.'

The deep sense of belonging and absolute commitment to the Project that they instilled is possibly one of the best examples of an orientation that focused on a 'cause' above all else.

Inducting Leaders on values is far more important than inducting 'normal Employees' on values. Leaders are expected to 'walk the talk' when it comes to values, and as such, ensuring potential Leaders are inducted into the corporate values as well as ensuring they truly live by them is important.

The more senior the Leadership position, the more important values become. Never forget that Leaders are role models for values and behaviours and are constantly under the microscope. One of the biggest reasons why organisations do not quite get their values propagated is because Leaders don't walk the talk – and the rest of the organisation sees this, and makes it the norm. Remember, the more junior positions 'mimic' the Leaders' behaviours. As such, the induction to values becomes essential if you want Leaders at the other levels of the hierarchy to take values seriously and live by them.

One of those extreme examples of Leadership positions being inducted for Values can be seen in the induction of College Prefects at S. Thomas' College Mount Lavinia, just south down the coast of the commercial capital Colombo.

The school, founded by Anglican Missionaries and modelled after Eton (where the founder Reverend James Chapman was an old boy), the school has a reputation for being a school of choice for many parents. Each year, there are over 2500 applications for less than 150 spots at kindergarten.

To be a College Prefect is the pinnacle of a student's career, and the 'badge' you wear from that day forth is something that one generation passes on to the other as an heirloom.

A Thomian Prefect's 'acceptance' into the 'Cop Shed[3]' is something that has been a guarded secret for generations which no self-respecting Prefect (current or past) will divulge. However, certain facets of it are public knowledge, which is all that needs to be shared to impress upon a ritualistic process to induct a Leader into Values.

One of the first things you go through is an initiation where the 'Seniors' invite each to-be-appointed Prefect into the room, interview them and ask them questions about how they would face certain situations. The Prefects are the ones who do the 'first screening' of the nominees and the 'interview' is attended by ALL Prefects. The focus on values is very clear – in fact, that is the only topic that the nominees are questioned about.

Students who have had 'blemishes' on their 'record' are quizzed about these, and asked openly about how they could 'instil discipline in others' when they themselves have transgressed. Students who have not had a 'squeaky clean record' are not dismissed, but offered an opportunity to 'redeem' themselves and the undertone is clear. IF they are to be made Prefect, they are DUTY BOUND to live the values.

Once the Prefects are chosen, on the very first day after they have taken 'oaths' at the College Hall in front of

3 Prefects' Room.

the entire school, presided over by the Warden and the Chaplain, the newly appointed Prefects are taken 'on parade' around the school. The new Prefects walk in front, and the Seniors follow. After this ceremonial 'walk' as the new Prefects, they are brought into the Cop Shed for the first time as Prefects, they take a second oath – one that has been designed by the Prefects of old, and passed down through each generation. This oath is fundamentally about three focus areas:

A. *To live by the 'Code' and not bring disrepute to the Prefects' Guild*
B. *To ensure that the Prefects act as one and remain a band of brothers, from that day till the end of time.*
C. *To ensure that the name of the College is never tarnished, and to ensure everything that is done is for the glory of the school, and not for oneself*

An integral part of the induction process is creating a sense of pride in the legacy. Every year, there is an Old Boys' Day. Here, the Prefects meet and greet great Leaders of yesteryear, and there is a unique bond that builds over time. Many are second, third, fourth, or even fifth generation Prefects. Yarns are spun, stories become legends, and tales of 'derring do' become part of the folklore.

At the epicentre is 'what it means to be a Thomian' passed down from generation to generation. The CORE of this entire elaborate scheme of things is to instil values – and ensure they are propagated – from one generation to the next.

There are three key lessons to learn from the S. Thomas' experience:

First, it is important for young Leaders to be 'vetted' by their peers. This becomes an induction even *before* they are appointed into positions.

Second, as much as the formal 'swearing in' of a Leader (by way of being given a Letter of Promotion, etc., and spoken to by the Senior Management) the informal 'pledge' they need to make to their peers becomes critical. This enables Leaders to work seamlessly across the organisation rather than in silos.

Finally, it is important to have a sense of belonging to a bigger legacy which is where stories, former role models and heroes all play a part. Organisations need to ensure that young Leaders are given a legacy to continue, not just a position to fill.

Another important element to be factored into the induction process for a Leader is an induction into the wider 'Leadership Team.' Far too often the challenge for many organisations is to get Leaders to work with other Leaders.

Too many times, egos get in the way and though teamwork is focused on *within* a department or unit, *collaboration* across the wider organisation is not the norm. However, the real benefit of Leadership is found when Leaders collaborate and work together – rather than working in silos.

One of the ways the LTTE fostered Leadership Teams was by getting newly appointed Leaders to go on extreme missions with their more senior counterparts. This achieved two ends: first, it enabled the bonding of Leaders, and it also offered an opportunity to learn skills and competencies from each other, enabling a healthy respect for each other (often, Juniors who had exceptional talent and skill were revered even by the 'Seniors' – and were supported wholeheartedly because their capabilities had been seen, first hand).

Some of the most covert operations, including that of the planning of and successful execution of the assassination of the then President Ranasinghe Premadasa, was given as a 'Project' to a Team that involved a cross-section of the Leadership brass of the LTTE. Many who were part of that Team remained true comrades till the very end.

So, in summary, what is critical is this: that Leaders are 'inducted' into their roles as Leaders, not just as Managers. There is a difference in the focus, and without it, all you have are Managers who think leading is 'by the way', rather than the core and primary role they have to perform.

The induction and orientation of a Leader as a 'process'; and not simply an 'event' that generally takes the form of a 'workshop' conducted by HR. It is essential that the induction and orientation of Leaders focus on a few fundamentals, and do this repeatedly rather than once:

A. Induction into the role of a Leader: what is expected, and why it needs to be differentiated from simply being a 'Manager';
B. Induction into the 'Vision/Mission' they need to be part of, and lead others in. This is critical if Leaders are to truly engage others in the journey;
C. Induction into the Values and why living values and being a role model for values is non-negotiable. It is essential that Leaders are told in no uncertain terms that violating values will be punished, and also may lead to demotions or dismissal (irrespective of how good a performer they are);
D. Induction with fellow Leaders and to working together. This can be augmented by training, but it is essential for the new Leaders to be brought into the fold of the 'Leadership Team' and it is necessary for them to 'get to know each other.' It would be a good idea to give a set of small cross-functional Projects for each potential Leader to do as part of their general orientation process, so that Leaders get to know each other, work with each other and also learn to respect each other.

Chapter 6

Supporting Growth

I have given you the best seeds, I have given you the best soil. You better make sure there are great yields. Or see farmers laugh at your face!

Emerging Leaders need to be supported if they are to blossom into Leaders who will ensure their organisation is propelled into the future. This support is fundamental, for without it, most individuals within organisations never quite reach their potential as Leaders.

What does support entail?

Support towards growing Leaders comes from four core elements:

First, through having Senior Leaders who are willing, and capable of mentoring and coaching their Emerging Leaders.

Second, having opportunities for Emerging Leaders to showcase their potential and learn from these experiences.

Third, creating exposure to different industries, organisations, and the opportunity to expand horizons.

Fourth, having access to specific development initiatives to enable new skill development and competency enhancement.

All these four elements are about having a culture of empowerment and introspection rather than fault-finding and finger-pointing. (We will look at each of these elements as well as more specific aspects of how Leaders can be 'developed' in the next section.)

Leaders need support to grow. There are always exceptions to the rule who will grow no matter where you place them, or the circumstances they are in. They are rare, and will excel irrespective of circumstances. However, most, will only truly fulfil their potential if they are supported and nurtured from an early age.

The reverse is also true. There will be those, who no matter how much you support, will not really make use of the opportunities and simply refuse to learn, grow, and take on more. These, you must have honest conversations with, limit to mundane routine tasks, and allow them to contribute in their own way – and, in some extreme cases, be removed from the organisation.

One of the unique features that is found in the paddy cultivation of ancient Sri Lanka that was forgotten in modern times (but still seen in some of the rural countryside) is the planting of 'Mee[1]' trees at the edges of a paddy field.

The 'berries' of the tree and the leaves act as an enriching fertiliser. This was one of the key reasons for the ancient farmers to yield bumper crops, that made Sri Lanka become known as the 'paddy store' of Asia and renowned for exporting paddy across Asia during the time of ancient Kings[2].

The British identified this as a 'threat' and supposedly systematically chopped off the trees over time.[3] This resulted in the gradual reduction in the harvest, paving the way for them to introduce chemical-based fertilisers which became the only way to have better yields, creating a dependency on imported fertiliser, something that is still the case.

Having a 'culture' where leaders are supported and nourished is ultimately what will ensure that Emerging Leaders grow within the organisation. Devoid of this culture, just like the '*Mee*' trees being chopped off, means creating impetus towards development being reliant solely on 'external' interventions, which are never sustainable nor fully capable of helping Leaders grow. It

1 Mee: *Madhuca longifolia* or Mousey Mi (English).

2 Especially during the Polonnaruwa era.

3 *Milestones in the History of Rice Improvement in Sri Lanka* – Dhanapala, M. (2020).

is important to understand that the 'nourishment' for the Leaders to grow is best when it is something internal, and something that becomes an integral part of the ecosystem of the organisation – not something that is 'added' periodically.

When support structures are not in place, two things happen. First, there is a widening gap in Leadership capability, competence, and skill between layers, and second, the best talent usually leaves. In many organisations where the ecosystem has not been able to grow Leaders at all levels, there is very little focused attention to acknowledge that Seniors need to take an active role in developing their next tiers.

In most organisations that have an ethos based on managerial structures rather than Leadership structures, the 'boss' and 'subordinate' relationship is all that exists, rather than a 'Leader' and an 'Emerging Leader' mindset. The 'apprentice'-type approach to developing your next level as a conscious decision one takes, and which becomes an integral component of one's job as a 'Senior' is not factored in, nor is it given any importance. All that matters is the business results and as long as 'Juniors' do 'what they are expected to do' everyone is blissfully happy.

The issue is that when Seniors 'retire', there is a massive gulf to fill, and often, talent is brought from outside and that 'culture change' that takes place becomes negative, destructive, and often extremely painful.

Many organisations never quite regain their former glory because continuity is hampered, and the organisation overall lacks the capability and bench strength of Leaders to continue to grow.

Maliban Biscuits is a brand that many Sri Lankans grew up with and was the market Leader in biscuits for over two decades. Founded in 1954 by Angulugha Gamage Hinni Appuhami, the small entrepreneurial venture became a powerhouse brand. The business also ventured into other lines of business over time. The core focus was always on the products. The focus on quality and distribution ensured that Maliban Biscuits became something of a phenomenon.

This supremacy and near market monopoly was challenged by Ceylon Biscuits Limited (CBL) who started to not only offer a wider variety of products but also, challenged the distribution penetration Maliban had established for decades. CBL also adopted a more corporate style of management, though they too were very much a family-run business.

The key difference was in developing management structures that established a much bigger focus on HRD and the development of core skills and competencies across the business.

With a Corporate and Cluster-based training and a development plan in place, the business focused on ensuring that each layer of management was given structured and ongoing development. This resulted in internal growth made possible for many Employees, and ensured there was enough management and Leadership bench-strength to support the rapid expansion of the business.

Compared to Maliban, who struggled to grow and sustain growth, CBL was able to grow fast and maintain the levels of performance year on year. Over a period of time, bolstered with some amazingly creative advertising and branding work, CBL became the Number 1 in the biscuits market and Maliban has never been able to regain its lost position for over a decade.

Maliban and CBL are great examples of how having a support structure to develop Leaders within an organisation plays a pivotal role in ensuring the business can grow and succeed in a sustainable manner in the longer term.

What is important to note is that 'creating an ecosystem' that helps Leaders grow within the organisation is as important as being able to bring top talent from outside, and often more so. Bringing talent from outside is important, no doubt, but too much of this does cause issues. People take time to settle in and move forward, and as such, ensuring there is a pipeline of Leaders, especially in the critical middle tiers becomes important, especially when scaling a business.

Part 3

Nurturing and 'Watching Over'

Once the paddy is planted, and the weeding done, there comes the longest period of the cultivation process: waiting for the crop to mature for harvesting. This is also the most decisive period, and there is a lot that can go wrong: from wild animals that can destroy the crop, to swarms of flies that can simply eradicate the crop in a matter of days, to untimely rain that can make the plants wither and die. This is also the time when patience is tested, and faith, hope and prayer are as integral a part of the process as is vigilant 'watching over' the crop – every night – until the harvest comes through.

This 'waiting period' is also a time when the entire village comes together to ensure the precious crop is protected. Elderly farmers resort to '*khema*[1]' rituals to ensure that no harm comes to the crop. However, it is not in ancient chants and 'magic' that they solely rely on. Far more 'practical' measures are taken to ensure that the beloved crop is safeguarded until they can harvest it.

The days start a little late during this period – as the nights are usually spent on top of a small '*massa*[2]' where farmers keep vigil to ensure no wild boar, elephants or other animals destroy their precious crop. It is usually customary to sing songs all through the night – 'tell tall stories' – and also – have a little '*ra*[3]' in moderation. These night vigils generally see the young ones being with their Fathers – and it is a time when 'wisdom' is shared from one generation to another. Stories of the best harvest and the 'tricks' they adopted to ensure the harvest is good, as well as stories of when 'disaster struck' and lessons learnt are told year after year. Before the British, much of tradition and practice was passed down

1 *Khema* – the closest translation is 'magic' – or ritualistic activities which are performed which the ancients swear by – and which has protected crops from insects and such for generations. Done right, the 'flies' that destroy paddy harvests never come – without any use of pesticides. This elaborate ritual is something of a dying art – but is still done in some villages. A chanted white thread is strung around the field – and it is ritualistically chanted on every night till the harvest ripens. Some villages have shamans who also do rituals if rains threaten – and the believers swear that the rain clouds part ways and never rains on the paddy field itself – even if it rains everywhere else in the village.

2 *Massa* – a small 'hut' built in the middle of the paddy field which is usually elevated to be able to see the entire field from a vantage point.

3 *Ra* – toddy made from either Kithul or Coconut trees – the local alcoholic beverage.

orally – from one generation to the other. This is one of the reasons why many of the age-old practices have died away with the generations past; especially because 300 years of colonisation also ensured systematic repression of the old ways, and many paddy farmers were almost forced to take on more modern ways, as well as changing trades altogether. A more burgeoning middle class saw a shift in the levels of importance given to traditional paddy farmers, and many of the next generations saw paddy farming as a lowly job: a stigma that still remains.

This period is when the next generation is prepped to take over from the elders. During the day it is common for farmers to sleep in a little, and then, during the day, teach the young ones about little tricks of the trade as well as ensuring the bulls and cows are tended for, rested, and prepared for the next season. They also ensure that the equipment they use is repaired, if necessary, new equipment bought or made, preparation for the harvesting is done, discuss prices with traders and ensure the '*Bissa*[4]' is repaired and if required, made anew. This period – when the plants were growing until harvest time - was also the time when the farmers spent a little more

4 *Bissa* – was a store room of sorts that almost all houses had in the front garden that stored the paddy for their own consumption. The '*Bissa*' was a unique architectural feature which ensured rats and other creatures could not get into it – and had just the right temperature and humidity throughout the year to ensure that the paddy did not rot or go bad. Paddy was threshed and made into 'rice' only as and when required – generally once a week. This way, the rice cooked was always 'fresh'.

time at home, rested, and also, looked after the other duties and responsibilities they had.

The usual 'day work' now turns to 'night work', and this shift in work patterns and times is something that the farmers do with absolute ease. It is also a time when they know they cannot do much by way of 'doing something' towards the growth of the plants – and so now, it is for the plant to do their thing – and grow – to their fullest potential. However, rather than using this time to simply idle, this becomes the time when farmers prepare for the harvesting, and ensure that their craft is passed down to the next generation. It is *not* in any way time they 'chill' – rather it is a time they invest in making sure the future of their beloved vocation is carried forward.

There are two key lessons to learn from the farmers about growing Leaders – and the 'nurturing' phase. First, as much as the farmers, you need to understand that your job is to allow the Leaders to grow – and that YOUR job as an organisation is to ensure they are given every conceivable opportunity to fulfil their potential. Once you have done your part, created the ecosystem and ensured the impetus is offered – you need to have the patience to 'wait' until you can 'harvest' their potential. The second is to understand that like the farmers, you have to 'make the time' to pass on the tacit knowledge – and keep the traditions alive through storytelling, rituals and also, active collaborations and gatherings. Growing Leaders – as much as farming – is very much a collective and communal exercise – and a cyclical one.

Chapter 7

Enabling the Gaining of Leadership Experience

"Never mistake knowledge for skills. Never mistake tenure for experience."

Leadership cannot be taught – it needs to be learnt. This is a fundamental principle we need to accept and acknowledge if we are to grow Leaders within an organisation. The primary focus needs to be on ensuring that Emerging Leaders are given the opportunity and the space to 'grow' in their 'experience' of Leadership – and a much lesser focus on 'training' *about* Leadership – which is also certainly necessary, but less so than creating learning environments for Leadership experience.

We learn Leadership by doing it – not by simply talking about it. We learn Leadership by being involved in the Leadership process – not simply critiquing it from the sidelines. We learn Leadership by both our successes and our failures – provided we are taught and coached to introspect and reflect. Experiences are things we all have – but learning from them is a skill that needs to be harnessed. What is *critical* is that we learn to *contextualise* our learning from our experiences rather than *generalising* them – which makes a huge difference in who we become as Leaders. Leaders who generalise their experiences tend to be fixed and rigid – and use their own experience as the biggest and fundamental barometer for future decisions – whereas those who tend to contextualise their learning are able to use their own experience as a starting point to a conversation and offer insights, rather than imposing a 'this is the way to do it' type approach to solving problems of a similar nature. *This* experience comes *only* if you are consciously driving *learning* from experience – rather than simply allowing experiences to be mere events.

Facilitating Leadership Development

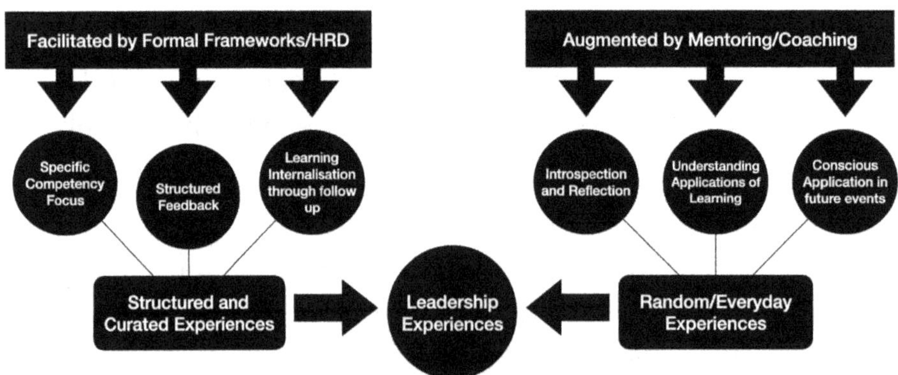

Emerging Leaders have a multitude of experiences each day. *All* of them can certainly be invaluable learning for Leadership. However, it is impossible to make *all* experiences something you *consciously* learn from. As such, being able to put a framework around the gaining of specific Leadership experiences is important in the development of Leadership and growing Leaders. Here, two distinct routes can be taken, each equally important.

Let's start with the Structured Approach. Curating 'Leadership experiences' can be done in three ways:

A. As part of formal training exercises
B. As exposure visits and follow-up
C. As distinctively different events/programs

Given we will be discussing the first two in more detail in other chapters, let's focus on curating Leadership experiences through a formal, structured, and curated event.

First, the starting point of the endeavour is to ensure there is a specific competency that is being looked at to develop. Once this is identified, it is important to structure an event around it. The event must be observed, and moderated, and learning culled out in a systematic manner. Furthermore, it must also involve a 'follow up' where the Participants can apply what they learnt in other settings – preferably in actual work environments, thereby demonstrating their ability to learn from the experience and also, replicate the learnings in different contexts. This is key. Simply learning something is *not* enough in Leadership – you must cultivate the ability to put learning into practice and get a result out of it. Learning for the sake of learning is fine in academic contexts; in work-related contexts, it is imperative that learning is the starting point of developing skills and competencies that enable you to lead better.

One of the most 'radical' experiences of a structured variety was a curated Program conducted in India which one of my friends attended (which has to remain anonymous for the purposes of confidentiality-related NDAs we have with our Client). A Salesman who was taking on the role of leading a Sales Team for the first time, was subjected to a 360 based on the Competency Framework of the organisation; and one key element that was identified was 'humility' and 'servant Leadership' qualities that were a definitive improvement area. During some of the focus group discussions that the HR Team did in identifying his areas for growth and improvement, almost all stakeholders noticed that he was extremely 'proud' and that he almost always wore his 'pride on his sleeve.' So, when he was to undertake a Leadership position for the first time, his immediate superior identified building 'humility' and the 'ability to serve' as that one area for improvement that would 'make all the difference' in his role as a Leader. One of the core Values of the business was 'humility' and 'treating everyone – and every job role – with dignity and respect'.

Rather than doing a traditional training Program per se, the intervention the organisation arranged was a brilliant example of a well-structured 'experience'-based learning opportunity.

My friend, along with a dozen others, was sent to India for what was described as a 'Development Exercise' with nothing more being briefed. On the first day of the 'Program' the Instructors gave them a small self-assessment, to assess their perceptions about 'serving', and what 'serving' entailed. Needless to say, everyone agreed that being able to 'serve' is important, both in sales and in Leadership. One question that was asked was: 'Can you be humble enough to truly serve?'; and the answer EVERYONE gave was 'YES.' The results of the 'survey' were projected; and when asked, 'Do you really mean it?', the entire audience exploded with a resounding 'YES!'

'Well – let's find out!' was all the Facilitator said. They were all taken out – and were taken to a set of public toilets. They were grouped into pairs, and each was assigned a 'Trainer' who was actually the person in charge of keeping each toilet clean. They showed them how the cleaning process is done, and told them that they were to ensure the place was kept clean for the day; and that each hour the level of cleanliness would be assessed.

Three groups took on the job, and got to work immediately. Two groups objected, but soon buckled down and got down to it. My friend flat-out refused, leaving his partner to do the entire chore, alone. When the first break happened for lunch, my friend still refused to clean toilets and simply told the Facilitator that he was 'not a coolie', and that his parents didn't educate him to 'wash public toilets – anywhere – least of all India.' There was a debrief at Lunch, and the Participants shared their insights. My friend sat with his arms folded, and absolutely fuming, he told me. He was completely insulted, and completely flabbergasted by the entire episode. However, listening to the learning experiences, he remembered his 360 feedback – and the one-on-one he had with his Immediate Manager and HR on the key areas for development. After lunch, he spoke to the Facilitator, and asked him if this was the reason they were given this task. The Facilitator simply explained, 'Your organisation lists dignity and respect for all jobs as a core value, and also, humility. How can you live by them if you don't really believe in them? What kind of a Leader will you be if you cannot truly empathise with the person who cleans the toilet in YOUR office? Think about it...'

My friend got on the job, and did the task assigned for the rest of the day. He tells me that he still felt angry – still felt it was beneath him – still felt rage – but he was able to rationalise his viewpoints about it; and realised with each passing hour that he was able to now truly,

truly understand what 'gutter level jobs' entailed, and the kind of stigma that was associated with them.

At his debrief, he recalled how lowly he felt when he settled into a 'sales job' because Sales at the time was considered the job you do when you could not do anything else. He spoke about the 'chip on his shoulder', about the need to prove himself, and that much of the accessorising he did, including the cufflinks he wore every day, the BMW he saved and saved and saved to buy – and the prestigious 'haunts' he would frequent - were all born out of that sense of 'inadequacy' he felt.

He tells me that he 'nearly cried' during his debrief: extremely uncharacteristic of his usually 'happy-go-lucky, come-what-may' attitude. That one experience was able to wake something deep within him, and transformed him to be conscious of his own hubris, and the need to humble himself and 'serve' as a Leader. He tells me that if not for that one experience, he would possibly be the 'biggest prick' as a Leader; and that the chances are the more senior he became, the 'bigger a prick I would have been.'

Upon his return, the 'change' was tracked through quarterly Reviews with the External Facilitator and also a Review with his Manager and a follow-up 360. There was a dramatic shift, and it was one of the things that his entire Team vouched for. Many of them wrote: 'He is a changed man'.

A well-structured experience can work wonders in enabling Emerging Leaders to introspect, reflect and internalise things that they would usually never do with traditional training or coaching interventions. Remember – the key is this – you need to 'experience' something – not only 'know about it' to truly transform.

It is also worth noting that though 'knowing about' Leadership is a cognitive exercise, 'experiencing Leadership' is very much an exercise that has an emotional connection. Unless you are 'moved' emotionally, all you experience is an intellectual stimulus – and it will simply remain just that. So, curating experiences needs to have structure to be effective and must:

- Be aligned to a definitive need (or gap in the individual) – connected to either the core competencies or values of the organisation
- Evoke an emotional response – coupled with guided introspections and reflections that enable the Participant to truly internalise the experience.
- Be followed up, to see if the internalisation reflects in the behaviour afterwards – and if the 'learning' is corresponding with 'changed behaviour' or 'results.'

Curating specific experiences to offer Emerging Leaders a space to learn and enhance their Leadership experience is not a cheap exercise – and it cannot be something that is done for everyone. Generally, such experiences are curated for identified talent pools - where the bulk of the investments are made (and rightly so.) However, it is important to understand that you cannot limit building Leaders to such events alone – as it is wholly inadequate to create an eco-system to grow Leaders. As such, it is important to ensure that everyday experiences are made use of, to ensure that Emerging Leaders internalise key lessons – and make them an impetus to grow as Leaders.

Towards creating a framework where 'learning' is a 'culture', two key imperatives need to be in place:

A. Individuals need to be 'taught' how to introspect and reflect
B. Managers need to be taught how to have 'meaningful conversations' with their Team members around everyday events and situations and experiences. Essentially, they need to be 'taught' how to be internal coaches and Mentors.

Unless individuals are able to intersect, reflect on and evaluate experiences they have, these are hardly 'registered' as a learning experience – and become merely a 'memory' unless you have someone to talk you through what to glean from it, and see different perspectives, the internalisation of learning becomes one-sided. So, when you can think through an event, and glean lessons from it, and you have others who will help you see some different perspectives and help you 'learn' from it – rather than simply being 'rewarded or punished' for it, what you are creating is that space for young individuals to experience Leadership lessons in everyday situations – enabling them to 'grow' with them.

There are plenty of opportunities within an organisation to offer young Emerging Leaders opportunities to experience Leadership and Leadership lessons. The easiest one to start with is giving them the opportunity to lead initiatives outside of their job scope and 'domain of expertise.' Many have asked me why you need to give something outside of their jobs – the reason is two simple things:

- Leadership needs to be differentiated from simply 'managing', and Leadership is *really* tested when they are outside their general comfort zones. Leadership is about the *person* as much as the task in front of them. Take people out of their comfort zones if you really want to teach them how to lead.
- Doing something in a different section or department helps them gain an appreciation for the wider business – which is invaluable when they become more senior within the business. Having done little

initiatives across the business gives them visibility to how other functions and Teams work – and builds a wider network within the organisation at an early stage in your career. This network and insight become critical for them to be an effective Middle Manager – and a Leader.

Pelemix is an organisation headquartered in Israel with branches and units in Sri Lanka, India, Thailand, Spain, and the US. They produce products made out of 'coir' or coconut fibre that are used for agricultural purposes. The biggest 'production' unit is based out of Sri Lanka where they have 3 core units employing over 500 people. An organisation that employs more than 90% of its workforce in 'blue collar' jobs, this is back-breaking manual work with very little by way of 'variation' and 'thinking.' How can you build Leadership pipelines for the junior levels in an industry such as this? Pelemix's example is a great opportunity to look at how 'everyday work' can be utilised to 'grow Leaders' across the organisation.

Pelemix introduced Lean Manufacturing Practices nearly a decade ago. Spearheaded by Namal – who started out as Manager of Process Improvement, and is currently the Acting COO of the Sri Lankan Operations – the Lean Implementation took a slightly different approach. Rather than teaching tools and going down the 'traditional' lean Six Sigma methodology, they adopted an approach to take a 'collective Leadership' approach towards ensuring everyone was involved in the changing of a culture – rather than looking at it as a 'Lean Implementation' per se.

Namal got their Supervisors to identify simple areas of improvement – based on their own observations and tacit knowledge ACROSS the business. He artfully ensured that he kept it open and inclusive – so that anyone could give a suggestion for improvement ANYWHERE in the business. The quality circles he formed were to attack SPECIFIC areas of improvement – and the 'Leadership' role was given to the person who brought forward the idea. This ensured that 'Leadership' was not something that was 'territorial' but rather, 'organisational.' The initiatives that were rolled out 'by the Teams – for the Teams' brought in amazing results – and also, many savings – most of which were used to offer better standards and incentives to the workforce – that created a ripple effect to improve things on an ongoing basis.

What was delightful to observe is that Namal took a 'coaching approach' (though he is NOT a certified Coach – nor had even HEARD of Coaching until we interviewed him about it as part of a development initiative we ran in the organisation many moons afterwards) towards making these 'initiatives' become 'experience building spaces' for Leadership development across the organisation. Many who were later promoted to more middle management roles were already seasoned 'Project Leaders' by that time, and, through them, developed a credibility that helped them move into more senior roles with ease. Whenever a new initiative was rolled out, three things were debriefed:

- *What went right – what went wrong*
- *What each person learnt about themselves*
- *Sharing of insights about each other – a Peer Review of what they thought each other could improve upon*

This 'learning space' brought in a culture of sharing insights, views, and reflections, and enabled each of the individuals who were leading Projects as well as supporting initiatives as a member of the Quality Circle to 'learn Leadership' without it ever being 'termed' a 'Leadership development initiative'.

The Pelemix example is a great illustration of how Leadership can be 'learnt' through 'everyday' activities and experiences – utilising opportunities to improve the organisation and giving opportunities to lead and learn through it.

Some key lessons:

- Initiatives were meaningful – and of impact to the overall organisation
- Leadership in the 'Circle' was given to those who brought in the viable idea for improvement – it was *not* based on 'seniority'
- Projects were given autonomy – and the Quality Circle *collectively* was held responsible for its success (or failure)

- The debrief was *not only* about the Project's success/failure – but about *what one learns from it*. It is important to note that feedback on how the individual led as well as feedback about each contributing member was shared openly, creating a collective learning space.

This way, even 'little' initiatives become wonderful opportunities to grow Leaders – across the organisational hierarchy – without ever having to spend money or take time off work. The everyday experience internalised in this way enables richer conversations and more meaningful observations of behaviour than any other possible avenue. It also means that you create a culture of learning whilst directly impacting organisational performance and growth.

Another great way of enabling learning from experiences is to look at great successes and failures as opportunities to learn from. Each of us goes through a multitude of experiences throughout a year at work – but we hardly make them opportunities to 'learn' from. Experiences we go through daily can be equally rich learning opportunities as conducting 'Special Projects' or 'initiatives.'

These learning experiences can be self-driven, but can be extremely effective if guided. Once again, it is essential for the individuals concerned to be 'taught' how to self-reflect and introspect, and equally important to teach the Manager how to 'Coach.' Whether they become formal or informal is a matter of personal choice.

Nimal Goonawardena is a veteran in the Advertising field in Sri Lanka. The former MD of the prestigious JWT agency in Sri Lanka, Nimal ventured out to start Bates Strategic Alliance and is currently the founder and CEO of his own boutique advertising and PR agency. Nimal was not the archetypical 'boss' and was very much a mentor to many who later became advertising giants in their own right. Something that I personally saw Nimal do was initiate and engage in 'informal' chats around 'incidents' at work.

Let me give you two illustrations.

Once, as a young newcomer who was an Account Executive, I made a horrible blunder with regards to an advertisement of a key client. The translation for an advertisement was wrong – and to add insult to injury – it was something that was so blatantly obvious that anyone should have spotted it. Understandably livid, Nimal blew off steam in the most expressive way, but, once he had 'cooled down' he took me and my Immediate Manager for a beer, and discussed three simple things:

- *WHY did this take place?*
- *WHAT needs to be done to ensure it is not repeated?*
- *HOW can YOU improve AS A PERSON?*

This was not a one-off occurrence. Whenever 'shit hit the fan' (his words - not mine) he would always take the time to do this reflection. In fact, I was once told by him to keep a 'journal of f@$ ups (again, his words, not mine) and WRITE what I need to do to improve – something I actually took to heart – and continue to this date. This simple ritual of being able to write and reflect on things that went wrong and what you can learn from this soon became a habit, which has enabled me to understand patterns of behaviour that I am generally unconscious of.*

On another occasion, we went in for a bid – a voraciously fought bid for a key client that Nimal was gunning for, over some time. Three years he lost it – but that year – the Team won the account. What was truly awesome was that Nimal was not part of much of the leg work (which he is very much involved in, hands-on under normal circumstances) as he was out of the island during that time. The 'pitch' went 'flawlessly' and there was a sense of jubilation in the office.

After much revelry, I remember Nimal summoning the entire Team together, and giving the Team that did the pitch the opportunity to share their learning from the experience with other Teams. Once again, he made them focus on three things:

- *How did they prepare for the pitch – what did they do differently from the other years?*
- *What can you replicate in ANY OTHER pitch?*

- *What did you learn about YOURSELF and your TEAM – and how can this be replicated when working on Projects?*

Notice, on both occasions, Nimal (who is also *not* a certified Coach – and Coaching was *not* a 'thing' 25 years ago when this episode happened) honed in on two very important elements in Leadership exposure:

A. He always brought in the 'what do you learn about yourself' element – making it about self-reflection – not only about 'what went right and what went wrong' and
B. He always prompted the Team to look at how it can be 'replicated' in other circumstances.

Ensuring that you learn from both success and failure is important. Whenever something goes right or wrong, if we are able to self-reflect – and understand what about us we can learn from it – and also, how we can take that learning towards other decisions we need to make or other incidents we are part of, what we are creating is an eternal learner within us. Reflection on and internalising of learning happen as a habit once you get into the groove of doing this regularly enough – and if you then supplement it with journaling these experiences, it becomes a transformative habit that will truly offer you the ability to become a much more self-aware and insightful Leader.

Nimal's approach to this was a very informal and often unstructured one. He was *not* doing this as a thought-through formal learning experience – he was doing it instinctively to get everyone to be more effective in their respective roles. However informal – the 'process' he adopted was something that could easily be replicated – and it was a process nonetheless. The constant reflection on things that went wrong and things that went right became something many in the organisation did in return, creating learning opportunities to not only learn from your own experience – but also from the experiences of others. The simple 'request' to 'journal' your reflections was not picked up by many – but those who did (like me) have benefitted hugely from it.

A more formal approach to the same 'process' was something MAS regimented. MAS sent their entire Senior Management Team to the prestigious Centre for Creative Leadership (CCL) to be trained formally as internal Coaches and be inducted into the Situation-Behaviour-Impact (SBI) model of coaching conversations. Once the training was completed, each Manager was mandated to have 'SBI' modelled conversations with their key direct reports every month – and look at one or a few key successes or failures and have coaching conversations around it. Though it must be admitted that not everyone did this as strictly as it was stipulated, many DID have regular conversations – which led to deep insights all around. This was further formalised by a written submission of key conversations on the Human Resource

Information System (HRIS). This regulated framework with a core structure institutionalised reflection-based conversations which was a gradual shift from 'finger pointing' to more constructive conversations around 'how can we improve.' Coupled with periodic 360s and development initiatives, both Managers and their subordinates learnt to self-reflect, get constant feedback and thereby, improve as Leaders in their own right.

Most of the Middle Managers and most Senior Management positions within MAS are filled internally, as compared to a decade ago – something that many attribute to MAS's deep focus on developing Leadership pipelines through investment and structured frameworks.

Another way to offer Leadership experience is to offer opportunities to expand exposure. This is usually done in three different ways:

- Exposure within the industry – within the wider organisation/group
- Exposure in related industries
- Exposure to completely different industries

Gaining exposure is critical for Leaders. However, once again, it is important to understand that 'exposure' visits per se are *not enough* to qualify as 'experience' – and once again, having structure and process is what makes the difference. As much as possible it is important to make sure the exposure visit is not a 'look-see' but an actual placement and if possible, a work-based arrangement for at least a few weeks. Being able to be 'placed' in a different environment and work and learn is invaluable learning – augmented a few folds if it is in a different country. Whether it is:

A. Curating the exposure visits with *definitive* learning outcomes and also, at least, an objective to implement at least *one* initiative that they will personally drive afterwards
B. Having inbuilt feedback loops from those the individual is working with
C. Developing a reflective mechanism – either through a journalling process or a regular meet-up to self-reflect with an internal or external Coach
D. Creating a Project plan framework for the initiative planned for after the visit
E. Implementing a feedback and reflection framework for the Project implementation phase.

Exposure visits are wonderful opportunities to broaden the horizons for Leaders – and to get fresh impetus about both technical and management initiatives in different companies/industries. However, whenever exposure visits are generally done, it is more with the intent of picking up best practices, rather than making use of it as a Leadership development exercise. This shift in focus is essential if exposure visits are to become more than simple visits to different places and picking up ideas to improve the organisation. Do not miss out on the opportunity to develop and augment Leadership through these exercises which often happen in many organisations without proper structures being put in place.

The Sara Lee Corporation is a Fortune 500 company with several different business divisions. Back in the 2000s, they bought over Courtaulds Textiles – the biggest apparel manufacturer in Europe at the time, making Sara Lee the biggest apparel manufacturer in the world. Courtaulds Clothing Lanka was a wholly owned unit of Courtaulds Textiles, which after the takeover, became part of the Sara Lee fold. Part of a much bigger corporation we at CCL (as Courtaulds Clothing Lanka was known) had a much bigger breadth of opportunity to get cross-exposure to different business units and learn from them.

Richard Cowlishaw was the then HR Director of Courtaulds Textiles, and my immediate superior on a dotted line – though my direct line of reporting was to the MD of CCL. One of the initiatives Richard implemented for us in HR was to enable learning of HR practices from across the divisions – including the Head Office as well as assignment-based activities in different countries where we were given the opportunity to gain exposure. It was an initiative that we undertook in earnest in our own HR unit – where we offered junior-level positions opportunities to hone skills through. Let me illustrate one such event.

Sajith Kethsiri was one of my two identified successors. Sajith was often referred to us as the 'Devil's Advocate' because Sajith saw flaws in anything quite instinctively. Though this irked us initially, his affable nature and good-tempered humour demonstrated to all of us that this was certainly 'nothing personal.' His 'unique instinct' to spot 'possible issues' or 'risks' saw him take to Risk and EHS[1] activities like a duck to water and he gained quite the reputation for being a diligent and painstakingly thorough assessor of risks. He soon became an Assistant Manager, and ensured that the organisation passed every single audit that took place (and we had quite a few) flawlessly without a single 'non-conformity' being listed. For Sajith to grow in his role, and in his Leadership capabilities exposure was critical – given that his only exposure to the function was within our fold.

So, with the blessings and initiation of Shirendra (our MD) and supported by Richard, we developed an 18-month plan for Sajith to gain much-valued insights. One of the initiatives within this overall plan was an assignment to get potential sub-contracting facilities identified and assessed for risks, and also, ensure they are guided to gain an 'all clear' from M&S[2] (our biggest customer at the time). Going to India for the first time, Sajith had to go and conduct a thorough audit process,

1 EHS - Employee Health and Safety.

2 Marks and Spencer – the British retailer.

then, guide the management Team there remotely, and do a final audit before the M&S audit to ensure there were no 'surprises.' Going into the assignment, Sajith was given a detailed framework of areas of focus – not only on the compliance and risk factors but also, on the key competencies he needed to focus on. Upon his return from the first visit, there was a series of feedback sought from the Management as well as the lower levels that Sajith worked with on specific competencies he was expected to grow in – specifically about his ability to influence, assert without 'bulldozing' and also, about his ability to find solutions collectively rather than 'giving' solutions.

Feedback collated was discussed with Sajith as a debrief, and further development areas were identified. A secondary feedback loop was factored in somewhere in the middle of his Execution Phase of the compliance execution process, and the final feedback was done after his final visit to India and the subsequent approval of the factory as compliant with the social compliance, and EHS standards stipulated by M&S. The final debrief with Sajith looked at his learning outcomes, and how he 'switched' his 'tactics' and how he had 'grown in maturity' as a Leader through this process.

Finally, Sajith was also given the task of implementing one thing that he thought was being done better at the Indian sub-contracting facility than at CCL. He had made copious notes about many different interesting practices and he took this opportunity to implement a series of improvements in our own facility, enabling us to win the coveted National Safety Award twice over consecutively, and also, becoming the first ever plant in the world to complete the combined World Responsible Accredited Production (WRAP)/Ethical Trading Initiative (ETI) certification.

The experience (one of many Sajith had) made Sajith the go-to person for all matters Compliance and Safety related, not only in Sri Lanka but also, even regionally. What made him a worthy contender was that he was not only a technical expert – but because he grew his Leadership skills to be able to work in different settings and play different roles with ease. He was identified as one of the possible candidates for a wider group-level role outside of Sri Lanka – and would have possibly got it, if not for the fact that he migrated to Australia where he currently resides.

Exposure is critical for the growth of Leadership potential in young Emerging Leaders – and must be taken on as a part of a structured development initiative. It should not be used as a 'reward' mechanism which many organisations make the mistake of doing. Sending someone abroad and giving them a 'tour' or a 'factory visit' as an 'exposure' does not really cut it as a development initiative. Many times, foreign visits are done as an 'incentive' for top performers – sadly – a structure around their development being coupled with it can make it a true investment in their development as well. What is worthwhile remembering is that we learn only when we introspect, internalise and *practise* what we learn. Without this framework and structure, no amount of exposure really registers within ourselves as a modality to grow. Rather, it becomes a lovely 'trip' we recall – never a lesson learnt.

Can you grow Leaders without all this structure and process or formality? Like plants – don't people naturally 'grow' with their everyday experiences and settings? Don't we actually grow *anyway*? We certainly do – In fact, many will argue that they had no real 'structure' around their development processes – that they were aware of. However, dig a little deeper and you will find that what they are referring to are 'formal' processes and 'frameworks' which we now refer to. However, many Leaders who have grown 'naturally' will tell you about great Mentors they had in their formative years, the 'opportunities' they were provided to grow, the 'challenges' they were given along the way and the 'support' they had from peers, friends, and superiors. The fact that it was not 'obvious' is not to mean the 'processes' were not at play, they were, albeit, informally, under the radar, not so obviously.

Developing Leaders must not be left to chance. Sure, we all grow in our own right. We all are capable of growth; we are all capable of reflection, introspection, and change. We are all capable of learning from our experiences.

However, if you are serious about growing Leaders at every level of the organisation, it is imperative to take a structured and conscious approach to it. It is too big a chance to leave it to 'chance' and 'eventuality.' Left to our own devices we may really never quite grow as *much* as we w ould if we were given tools, opportunities, advice, required nudges and those all-important opportunities to learn.

The critical part is this. *Anything* and *everything* can be a learning opportunity but *only* if we *know* how to *learn* and *glean* the required lessons from it. Learning is not a simple process - nor is it something we all do enough of. Having frameworks and structures to ensure that learning becomes an integral part of any experience is something that needs to be *cultivated* in us. If this is done, early on in our careers, we become lifelong students of Leadership – something that is critical if true Leadership potential is to be harnessed.

Chapter 8

The Role of Mentoring and Coaching in Growing Leaders

"Children may not listen to what you say but they do observe intently what you do and what you don't."

By now it must become obvious that if Leaders are to grow within organisations, having Seniors who are great Mentors as well as Coaches becomes quite essential. In fact, possibly the biggest way young Leaders are grown is under the tutelage of Seniors who become role models.

Before we proceed on how to build great Mentors and Coaches – and how they can be used to augment future Leaders, let's differentiate between Mentoring and Coaching. Mentoring is when a senior guides and directs a more junior employee. Mentors and Mentees are almost always inside the organisation. Coaching is when you work with an individual to help them grow in a specific aspect. Mentoring and Coaching are *both* focused on the individual's development but with a stark contrast in approach. Mentoring is *directive*, whilst Coaching is *collaborative*, and the Coach is there only to *guide* the coached discover the solutions themselves. Mentoring will *tell*, Coaching will *discuss*. Mentors use their own experience and tacit knowledge to give you solutions; Coaches are trained in having conversations that enable you to discover alternatives and options by yourself. *Both* arrive at conclusions, *both* help you grow – but in very, very different ways.

Today, most organisations (and popular management literature) place a lot more emphasis on Coaching than on Mentoring. In fact, it is quite common to downplay the importance of mentoring with a much bigger favourable bias towards coaching. This I believe is a huge mistake; both are needed for Leaders to be grown within an organisation. One without the other leads to misaligned Leaders.

It is certainly true that Leadership is a transferable skill – and that you do not need to be a technical expert to lead a Team of technical experts. Being able to 'lead' them is a wholly different skill from being able to do each of the jobs your Team does better than they do. This concept however is a double-edged sword. Many times, *not* being technically sound is something that leads to disastrous results, especially in specific industries where technical ability and know-how are essential in solving complex problems and issues that crop up. Simply 'huddling' and 'figuring it out together' is not an option at times – and in these crucial moments, being able to be technically competent enough to *ask the right questions,* and thereby arrive at possible solutions, is a critical skill to have.

This is why Mentors are critical at an early stage in your career and to grow Leaders at the early stages. Because of our misunderstanding of the role of Mentoring and Coaching, there is a reluctance amongst many Senior Leaders to *direct* their Juniors and give 'marching orders' – preferring to take the more 'coaching conversation' route.

So, understand that Mentoring is indeed needed and is *not* alternated with or replaced by or substituted by Coaching.

- A Mentor *knows exactly what to do* in certain circumstances. This is critical in technical aspects – and no Coach (especially from outside the organisation) can give you this level of in-depth insights and definitive solutions
- A Mentor has 'been there and done that' – his/her approach is not a 'let's figure it out' approach – he/she has already figured it out. Your learning curve is crushed when you work with a great Mentor.

- Working with a Mentor also enables you to work at a very different 'level' of performance. Mentors are usually much more Senior than you – and there *are* expectations of you (unlike a Coach who is your guide and has no 'expectations' of you per se – apart from the development they want to see). Mentors generally have definitive 'targets' for you – and working at that pace will help you grow – and stretch yourself.
- A Mentor also has significant power over you. This necessitates you humbling yourself to take 'instructions' and 'orders' from them. A coaching relationship is *not* power-based. The experience is wholly different.

So a mentor sounds like a horrible idea? Well, in many cases Mentors are tough, demanding and extremely pointed, but it is not always the case – there are plenty of pretty 'cool' and 'chilled out' Mentors too. However, the vast majority of *really good* Mentors have just one thing in common – and it is *not* their approach or personality or their affability (or lack of it) – It is that *great Mentors know their stuff* and they are *willing* to teach you *all they know*. They generally share another trait: most of them will *not bother* with you if you are *not willing to learn on their terms*. Great Mentors don't want to waste their time with those who only pay lip service to 'I want to learn' – they often put you through proverbial 'shit' simply to discern whether you *really* want to learn.

So, be warned that being Mentored is *not* easy; but it *is* invaluable.

What *is* useful is for those who are identified as Mentors to be given some training on Coaching too. This certainly helps. *Knowing* the Coaching Process and being conscious of the 'other way' of helping young emergent Leaders helps Mentors mentor better. However, once again, many of the great Mentors will possibly not really care too much for the 'preference' of 'learning styles' or 'how they need to be given feedback' – they will simply argue that 'if you are serious about learning, you will come and take it, if you are not, you will drop out - that is completely up to you.'

Identifying Mentors becomes essential for an organisation serious about growing Leaders.

- Identify those who are 'damn good' at what they do.
- See if they are 'technically competent' as well – or whether their performance comes out of other aspects – such as having a great Team, a generally positive market place, etc.
- Assess their ability to *teach* – and their *willingness* to teach as well.
- Understand what *kind* of person is best *paired* with the individual – there really is no point giving a good Mentor a Mentee who is a 'bad fit.' A simple personality test or preferred teaching method type test paired with the preferred learning method test for a Mentee should be able to give you a good idea of how to pair a Mentor and a Mentee.

Pairing Mentor and Mentees

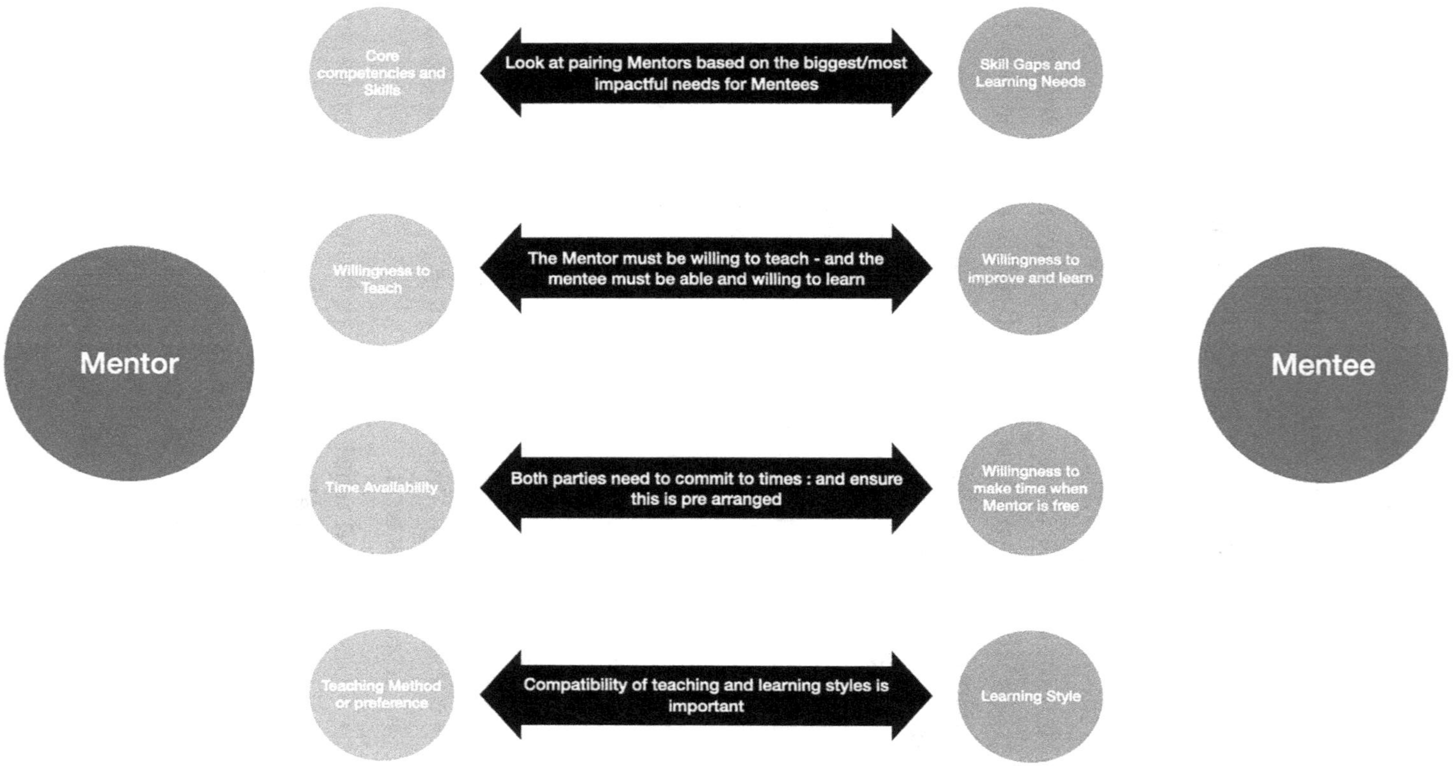

Mentor

Mentee

Mentor		Mentee
Core competencies and Skills	Look at pairing Mentors based on the biggest/most impactful needs for Mentees	Skill Gaps and Learning Needs
Willingness to Teach	The Mentor must be willing to teach - and the mentee must be able and willing to learn	Willingness to improve and learn
Time Availability	Both parties need to commit to times : and ensure this is pre arranged	Willingness to make time when Mentor is free
Teaching Method or preference	Compatibility of teaching and learning styles is important	Learning Style

Once you choose the set of Mentors, it is important to ensure there are frameworks around the Mentoring Program as well. Generally, Mentoring happens 'by chance' where Seniors who take a certain liking towards certain Juniors take the time and the effort to 'groom' them 'under their wing.' This happens in almost every organisation anyway, but is not enough if you really want to 'grow' Leaders across the board. Mentoring is far too important to be left to chance – and Mentoring, done early in a career, can, and will make a huge impact later on in careers. So, take the time to set up the Mentoring Processes and Frameworks – so that it happens consistently, and productively.

- Have a Mentor induction Program. Explain the role of a Mentor. Take the time to take the Mentors through the Mentoring Process – and also – the critical dos and don'ts. Remember to set the expectations right – and explain the criticality of Mentoring in key areas for the overall business to grow – and for succession to be created. Also, ensure the Mentors understand that what they do is considered important within the organisation.
- Have a Mentee Induction Program. Ensure Mentees understand that this is *not* coaching – and that the Mentors' time is given voluntarily and as such needs to be respected and valued. Ensure the Mentees understand that this is not a 'free ride' and that they need to commit to it.

- Have a common 'get to know your Mentor/Mentee' forum and evening/event. Get the Mentors and Mentees to meet and greet, get to know each other and discuss their expectations openly.
- Have a format for Mentors and Mentees to follow so that there is uniformity in *how* the Mentorship works. Make sure there are guidelines on:
    - Meetings – and scheduling
    - What to discuss – and how to make notes
    - Documentation of discussion points for future reference
    - Mapping of progress being made – and guidelines on how to measure and monitor progress
    - How to discuss concerns or setbacks or the need to exit the Program for whatever reason
    - Have a measurement of success for both Mentors and Mentees
    - Have regular feedback from both Mentor and Mentee
    - Have an independent party to settle any major conflicts that can happen

Remember – getting a Mentoring Program to work is crucial. Because, unlike a Coach who can be brought in from outside, Mentors are almost always internal. Therefore, if the Mentoring relationship does not work, there is every possibility that it will affect their normal work relationships inside the organisation. So, if you are putting effort into making a Coaching framework work – put double effort into make a Mentoring Framework work – because there are more risks involved in Mentoring than with Coaching.

Your Immediate Manager being your Mentor for Technical aspects is often inevitable. Most Middle Managers are promoted for technical competence rather than Leadership competence – and it is only after that first-tier promotion that most organisations put more effort towards Leadership Capabilities. As such, most of the time, for technical functions, the Mentor inevitably becomes your own Line Manager. However, for other areas of expertise, anyone from across the organisation can be a Mentor. When preparing Mentoring Frameworks, pay special attention to the organisational dynamics too, because it will be rather naive to ignore them.

Mentoring comes in handy at three distinct stages in the career of a Leader:

A. When you start out – especially if you are new to the industry – to understand the role and the 'ropes' quickly and quicken your learning timelines considerably, a good Mentor really helps. This can often be a peer – or your Line Manager.

B. As you move into the first Leadership role, a Mentor to help you come to grips with the role as a Leader and, understand the subtle yet rather deeply impactful shifts you need to make in both your attitude and your behaviour, becomes important. Skip-Level Managers are usually awesome for this role – as are some well-respected Senior Leaders within the organisation.

C. The next phase when you really need to be mentored is when you take on a more 'general management role' rather than a functionally senior role. General Management necessitates that you take over functions for which you have little or no professional qualifications, no experience, or are located in areas in which you have never worked. This is when you need Leadership *most* – to be able to navigate technical waters without expertise – and this is when you need a great Mentor the most too. Here the Mentor will teach you how to ask the right questions so that you are never quite 'taken for a ride', intentionally or unintentionally.

Having a structured framework to look at the distinctive needs at each stage of a young Leader's career, and having Mentors lined up for it on an ongoing basis helps have continuity to the Mentoring process, and also, makes it seamless rather than 'even based.' Mentoring should not be considered annually per se – rather, it is best when it takes the whole lifecycle of an employee. Being able to look at the 'gaps' in 'competencies' on an annual basis is important – but the pool of Mentors and the frameworks need to be in place for longer durations – and adjusted annually.

A few other considerations:

- Ensure there are enough Mentors to go around. Never overburden one person – this generally becomes counterproductive.
- Link mentoring progress to both the Mentor's and the Mentees 'appraisal' (not the 'performance appraisal' but the 'development appraisal'.) Make sure that the progress of Mentees is linked to their 'potential' being assessed – and the readiness thereof for more senior roles, and the impact Mentors make linked to their 'ability' to grow others – which in turn is linked to their advancement to more Senior Management roles. Make 'mentoring' and 'grooming successors' a factor to consider when promoting Senior Leaders (which we will discuss in detail in a later chapter)
- Be able to remove Mentors who are ineffective. Similarly, be able to not invest in Mentees who are not really putting in the time and the effort to make use of the mentorship. Both need to have a penalty system – which ideally should be linked to their career progression (once again, discussed in more detail in a later chapter).

Something to also consider is this: Mentoring helps the Mentor as much as the Mentee. Mentoring helps hone skills for Mentors – especially with regards to being able to 'teach' others, thereby helping develop a healthy pipeline of technically competent, well-rounded Leaders

Creating Mentor Mentee Synergies

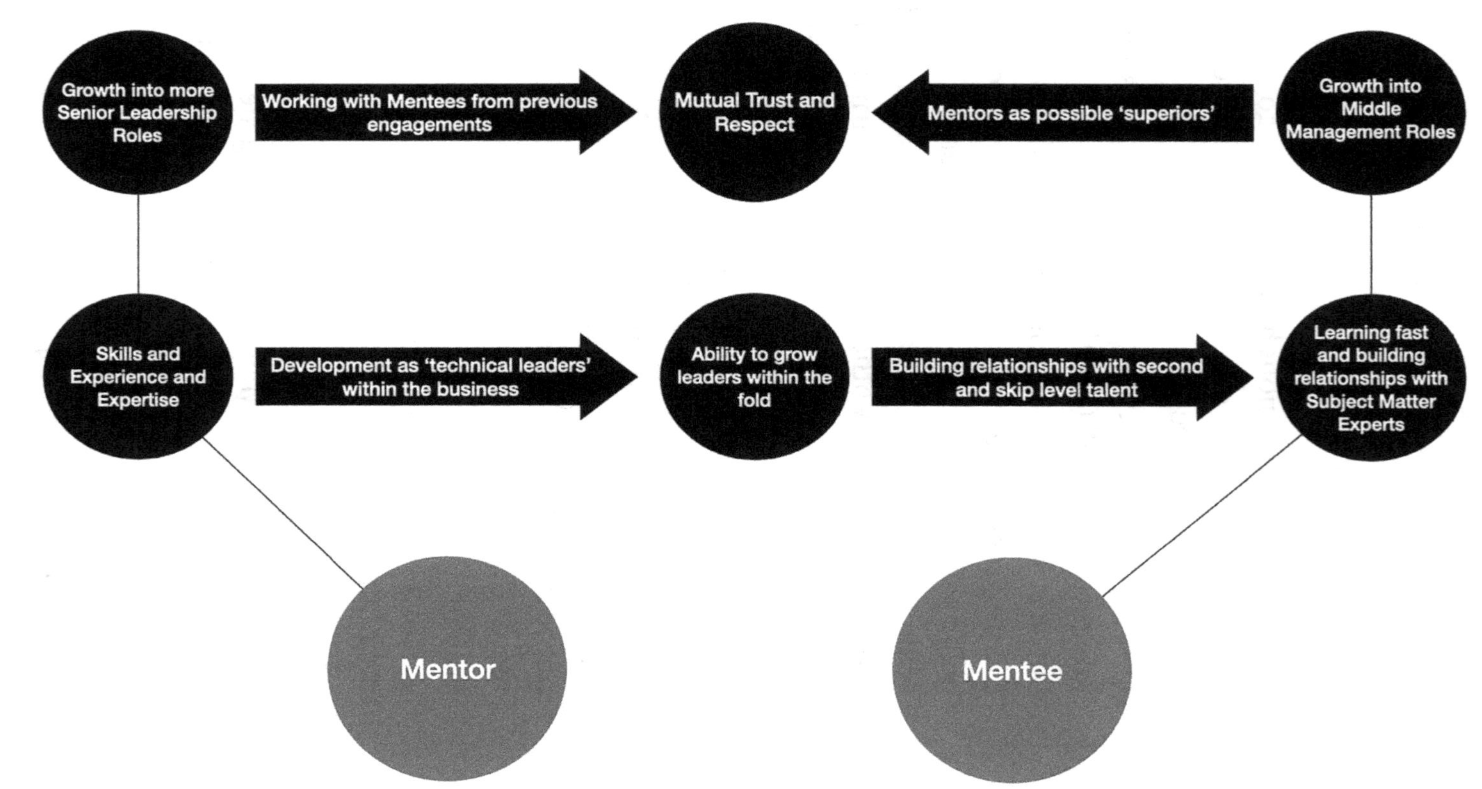

in their own departments. Having a solid Team with good depth helps any Senior Leader perform better, so actively engaging and developing talent across the hierarchy helps Senior Leaders ensure they have solid Teams that can offer superlative performance without having to micro-manage. It also gives them the opportunity to assess and get to know the talent pool within their own Teams, and, across the organisation, enabling them to understand who can be shifted where, based on the talents identified. Mentors gain insights into people that would otherwise be impossible in larger organisational settings.

A solidly designed Mentor Program enables the development of a healthy ecosystem for the development of both Emerging Leaders as well as ensuring more Senior Leaders are inducted into the role, they must play in 'growing Leaders' as part of their central function as a Senior Manager. Having Mentors from the Middle and Senior Tiers enables the organisation to have a cross-fertilisation of skills and competencies and build a healthy relationship with skip levels early on in the careers of the top talent of the organisation. Overall, a well-formulated and executed Mentoring Program will help everyone – and it will help a much deeper mutual respect between the tiers. A Mentor who helps a junior forge forward wins amazing respect internally, and a Mentee who makes use of the mentorship and propels forward wins a huge amount of respect from Seniors. So, use mentoring Programs to build a 'Leadership ecosystem' across the board at all levels.

The inspiration for the frameworks for Mentoring came from observing an iconic 'eatery' in Colombo

Raheema's in Colombo is the stuff of legend and has been a place where generations of schoolboys and patrons from all walks of life came in for a meal. The establishment is well over 100 years old and is situated right opposite Thurstan College – a popular school in the heart of Colombo. Famous for its Parata and Beef Curry in the mornings and Roast Chicken Biriyani for lunch, Raheema's is not just an eatery: it is a landmark and a 'tradition.'

The waiters who work there have been there forever – and the 'new ones' are as affable and customer-centric as their predecessors. The distinctive taste of the fried beef, the roast chicken and the well-kneaded Parata has remained the same – certainly for the 30+ years I have been walking through its doors.

How they pass down tacit knowledge, and 'groom' those who come in new, is something I got interested in when I observed a few 'new recruits' as waiters – and when my interest was piqued as the old waiter who was an icon already within the establishment inquired about the food for the first time one day. I asked him why he asked me about the breakfast – which never happens. He smiled and told me it was a 'young cook' who was cooking for the first time that day. I had not noticed the difference – and the old timer was happy – going into the kitchen with salutations and praises in Tamil. I went into the kitchen with him afterwards (not exactly ISO and HACCP certified stuff here – In case you are getting ideas to visit it too!) And from that day forth, ever so often I ask the waiters if the cook is the same. During the time I have been patronising the place – they have changed cooks five times (one lasted only six months – the shortest stint a cook has done in the place) and apart from just twice – I would not be able to tell the difference in the food for the decade I consciously tried to see if I could spot a difference.

(I would eat from Raheema's weekly – religiously – whilst I was in Colombo! It is something I inducted the entire family into. After a good walk in a nearby ground, I would take my entire family to Parata, Beef Curry, Dhal Curry, Fried Potato and Chicken Curry – my wife does not eat beef – topped with a strong tea for everyone – apart from my wife who does not drink tea - and as such, has a fruit juice instead!)

So, how do they do it? How do they make sure the food AND the service are of consistent quality for generations (my uncle before me was a Raheema fan – visiting it almost daily as a student of Royal College, and then, as an Undergraduate at the University of Colombo.)

Raheema's secret is simple. The key recipes are NOT written down – would you believe it – each is passed down from one cook to another by a rather serious 'mentoring' process. First, the choice of the cook is NOT down to the owner. The owner brings 'helpers' and from the 'helpers' the 'cook' (there are no 'chefs' in Raheema's) observes and chooses someone he deems worthy to be his successor. The chap – who is generally young - is then inducted into doing all the cutting and chopping – a step up from the cleaning job they are generally given first. He is then brought in to help with the cooking – and finally given the charge of cooking under the tutelage of the senior. They almost always have two cooks as a minimum (generally three) ensuring there is always a contingency, and each cook generally has three 'understudies' – one each – and each 'understudy' generally has someone under them, too. So, at any given time, there is ALWAYS someone who can take over and they are each capable of cooking those 'special' dishes that Raheema's is synonymous with, to absolute perfection.

Here is where things get really interesting; There is an unwritten rule that unless your junior can do the dish to the right level of perfection you are not worth your salt as the cook – and in the kitchen, this is a matter of intense pride. This is why the waiters ask us whenever a new cook is taking over – and offer that feedback to the cooks – as there is a sort of 'competition' to see whose 'junior' will be the 'best.' This sense of pride in teaching the next generation – and a deep sense of duty towards propagating what they consider their 'legacy' makes the Mentoring 'process' something akin to the 'apprentice' of a bygone era. The apprentice was considered the 'legacy' of the 'master' – and so it is at Raheema's too.

The 'training' of the waiters is the same. There is a grand old man at Raheema's who has been with the establishment for over fifty years – from the time he was a young boy! He knows almost everyone who frequents Raheema's – and knows what each patron wants as soon as they walk in.

If ever I walk in with my family – he knows what we want – and he knows the 'order' is very different if I go in with my work colleagues. This level of intimacy is something we 'expect' from Raheema's – and he knows it. Whenever a new waiter comes in – he (and two others who are as tenured as him) takes over them. They generally bark out orders to them during their formative days and then observe them like hawks. You could see them getting the new recruits to 'hurry up' with hand gestures and stares and, if someone stepped out of line, you could see one of them taking the young buck into the kitchen for a good 'earful.'

What is rather awesome to see is when the 'rush hour' diminishes, they sit them down for a tea – and share stories – and insights – and almost daily – a 'debrief' about what they had done right and what they had done wrong. This constant feedback and definitive 'instruction' on the 'dos and don'ts' ensures that each waiter – though having their own unique personality and quirks – has the same fundamental focus on customer intimacy the establishment has been known for.

Observing Raheema's over the years I made a framework to induct, orient and mentor top potential candidates for a few of our clients over the years. Getting some of my colleagues to observe this process is also something I have incorporated as their 'training' in being able to identify 'management lessons' from the most unlikely of 'sources.' The 'illustration' in this section was penned over a decade ago after discussions with the 'old chaps' whilst having breakfast one day – prepping to develop a policy-level framework for one of my clients.

An interesting 'twist' to Mentoring for Leadership development is the process of 'Reverse Mentoring.' Mentors are usually 'Seniors' and the 'mentee' is usually a 'junior.' Reverse mentoring is when a 'junior' Mentors a 'senior', which is a brilliant way of introducing a more egalitarian learning culture into the organisation. Reverse Mentoring also establishes the much-needed ethos that learning – especially for Leaders – is something that must be considered on merit – rather than on 'position.' Having a Reverse Mentoring process places the 'forcing' of individuals to humble themselves to learn from 'anyone' – an integral part of Leadership development – and a pivotal cornerstone of a true Leadership-rooted culture.

The reality is that there are many in the Junior ranks who are equally skilled or are more skilled than those at

Senior levels at different competencies. Rank or Tenure is *not* an automatic barometer for competency or skill – and identifying those who are competent or skilled across the organisation – irrespective of their 'rank' – and using them to 'train' others break the traditional hierarchical boundaries within the organisation – forces the organisation to embrace a more egalitarian approach fundamental to the growth of Leaders across all levels.

Being able to teach as a Leader is important. So is being able to learn from anyone. At more senior levels, Leaders who are able to humble themselves to learn from anyone and anywhere are critical – especially for their growth as Senior Leaders. Towards this, a reverse mentoring process is a great tool to use.

One of the most impressive Reverse Mentoring initiatives that I have seen was at Phoenix Industries. Phoenix is one of the biggest (if not the biggest) plastic manufacturers in Sri Lanka – and a household brand with a huge reputation for quality and durability. With cheap imports flooding the market from India and China, the traditional product range with which Phoenix used to dominate the market was being eroded, and many of the traditional products they made were becoming unprofitable. The business suffered losses for nearly half a decade, and on a few occasions the family discussed the very real possibility of selling the venture – though they never did – mostly due to nostalgic rather than business reasons.

In 2004, they brought in a new CEO – Hasith Premathilake. A qualified engineer and finance professional, Hasith was brought in from one of their key customers – CALTEX – and charged with turning the business around. There was one BIG problem though – Hasith was NOT from the Industry.

Aslam Omar – the MD of Phoenix – got Hasith to understudy and be 'Reverse Mentored' by several key 'old hands' (three of them were not even from the Management tiers) so that Hasith was 'technically sound.' Given that Hasith was an Engineer made this process relatively easier – but, the formal assignment of mould changers, technicians and even a salesman (who did the retail sales) to 'Mentor' the new CEO and ensure he was properly inducted and trained about the industry, enabled the entire organisation to understand that learning was not something that was hierarchy-driven. It also helped the new CEO understand the subtle nuances – and the inner dynamics of the Teams – not just the technical know-how.

Each week Mr Aslam would 'grill' Hasith on technical aspects – and if he did not really know the 'answers' – he would take this up with his 'Reverse Mentors' and charge them with 'teaching the boss better.' This 'tradition' was something that became a norm after some time – and even today – it is common for the 'technicians' to 'teach' the young graduates who come in, who later become their superiors.

This process has also led to a very healthy respect the 'Managers' have for their technical staff – and also – a very real appreciation for their experience and exposure over the years.

Coaching thankfully has gained a lot more focus and 'interest' in Leadership development these days. There are also definitive frameworks that have come out that help an organisation 'plug and play' Coaching into their HR and related development frameworks.

However, something I observe is that Coaching too is something that is being considered by many as something that happens as 'events' rather than an integrated framework that becomes part and parcel of the development ethos of the organisation. Coaching is fast becoming something that is done for 'top talent' and 'fast-tracked' individuals – rather than something that is done for everyone – as a matter of everyday practice – as a function of management and learning.

Once again, the issue is that there is far too much emphasis on Coaching as a 'formal' exercise – and far too little focus on making Coaching a 'way of life' within the organisation – which is where I think the bigger benefits come from, overall. This is *not* to negate the absolute importance of having specialised Coaching interventions for specific areas of development for specific talent pools. This is to bring to the fore that Coaching needs to be an integral part of the development dynamic – NOT an event that happens for a small group of people at a predetermined time and for a set duration as part of the 'training calendar.'

The type of Coaching required for each layer is different, especially with regard to building Leaders itself.

Senior Levels

A. Senior Leaders need to have definitive Coaches who are external to the organisation, who will help them become architects of ecosystems that will help them create the kind of culture that is required for Leaders to be grown at all levels. This is often something that cannot be done internally per se – and it is also important to consider this exercise as a 'group' coaching type arrangement. This way, all Seniors have a common understanding of the role they need to play – and also – very importantly – the framework they need to *jointly* put in place to ensure Leaders are grown within each tier of the organisation. This Coaching is fundamentally different to individual development-based coaching. This type of coaching is often sadly missed in most organisational settings.

B. Seniors will also need to be coached on specific Leadership competency gaps, which can be coached either through an internal or external Coach.

C. Another important consideration at Senior Levels is to ensure they are coached to *become* coaches in their own right. This is also important. Seniors need to play the coaching role for both their immediate Juniors as well as skip levels – and at times – laterally to peers.

If Seniors are coached to become Coaches, coached to build effective Leadership ecosystems and are helped through their own development, you enable the building of a Senior Tier that understands not only their role as Leaders but also, the prime levers they need to move, to ensure Leadership is grown within the overall organisation. This is key. Never look at Coaching only as the development of an individual per se – especially at Senior Levels, look at the holistic development of a Leadership Team and a Leadership Ecosystem through Coaching interventions.

Middle Levels

Realistically, whatever strategies are conceptualised and agreed to are charged with being 'executed' through the middle tiers. The Middle Management tiers are also critically important as a 'go between' the 'Seniors' and the 'rest of the organisation.' In most organisations, the middle management tier is where Leadership is in most need of augmentation.

A. Coaching on the role of being a Coach to your own Team, which is important as a Line Manager. This can be done either as a Coaching Certification Process – or better still, as a hand-holding process through either an internal or external Coach who has gone through the process personally

B. Coaching on specific competency gaps, where Middle Management Leaders need to improve in order to move forward in the hierarchy and take on more senior roles within the organisation

At Junior Levels

At the more junior levels, it is critical that the Emerging Leaders are coached by the Immediate Managers – and possibly Skip-Level Leaders. Coaching by external coaches is to be considered only in specific and exceptional circumstances – if at all – for those identified to be fast-tracked.

A. Competency Development – should be the primary focus. Given that the immediate Line Leaders will be working with them on a regular basis, ensuring that the coaching methodologies are adopted to ensure that they are groomed and grown (as opposed to vindicated and found fault with) is critically important.

B. Performance Enhancement – should also be a definitive focus – given that this is where most of the key challenges come in from between Line Managers and their subordinates. Adopting a coaching approach to performance enhancement enables the development of a much healthier and respectful relationship between Line Managers and their subordinates – and the Emerging Leaders get a firsthand experience of how *they* need to act as Leaders when they come of age.

Creating a Coaching Culture within the organisation is fundamental to growing Leaders. Far too often, performance is considered separately from behaviour – which is a big mistake. Performance – especially if you want to have a Leadership-focused organisation – must always be *with* people – rather than at the *cost of* people. Being able to drive performance without the typical micromanagement and heavy-handedness requires all levels to embrace a coaching approach.

Developing a pool of Coaches becomes important for the organisation. Both internal and External Coaches need to be chosen with care – using a similar framework that has been discussed in the section on Mentoring. Though each Line Manager is *expected* to be a Coach too – it is important to factor in compatibility and related aspects when Coaching is considered as well. Though for everyday performance-related conversations, the basic Coaching frameworks are more than enough – for more specific individualised competency enhancement-related Coaching, ensure you take the same approach discussed in the Mentoring Framework. Remember – a Coach and a Coachee have to be in sync as much as a Mentor and a Mentee.

Another vital factor to consider is choosing external Coaches to help you. Do not take this decision lightly – as Coaches play a pivotal role in the development of your key Leadership bench strength. So, the 'recruitment and orientation of' the Coaches play a significant role in whether the Coach truly adds value to the process or not. If you are going through a rather structured process to recruit at any level, should there not be a more rigorous process to select and induct those who will be in charge of developing your Leaders?

Select a few Coaches per tier, if possible, just one. The 'consistency' of what is being coached and the process adopted is important in having a certain semblance of uniformity in how individuals are developed within an organisational setting. When you have a multitude of Coaches, it is common for very different forms of approaches to be taken – and those being coached are assimilated into this 'ethos' and 'framework.' Having a uniform approach helps individuals within a tier relate to each other – and their learning experiences.

- Select a Coach who has had similar challenges, experiences and contexts. Coaching is *not* mentoring – granted – but being able to empathise with contexts is critically important to ensure there is no disconnect between Coach and Coachee. Many times, Coaching fails because there is a disconnect in the ability to contextualise.
- Ensure all Coaching is pegged to *deliverables* – and

not just timelines or vague expectations. Be *specific* about the improvement area – and ensure that this area is in turn pegged to one of the Leadership competencies listed for the tier.

- Induct and Orient the Coach to the business, the Vision, Mission, Values, Strategies and the Competency Framework of the organisation. Though an external resource, it is important that the Coaches bind with the overall organisational ethos of the organisation to be effective as developers of Leadership within your organisation's fold.

Coupled with structured Mentoring, a solid Coaching Framework and Culture is a potent combination to help grow Leaders at all levels of the organisation. Unless Coaching becomes an accepted 'norm' in shaping the way 'conversations' take place, the drive towards performance often becomes toxic and detrimental – and there is a gradual erosion of mutual respect, values and, the overall focus on developing Leaders (with a heavy bias towards simply ensuring 'performance' happens – no matter what the cost.)

Chapter 9

Formal Leadership Development Training Programs

"The onus of teaching is the teachers; the onus of learning is the students."

Leadership Development Programs are possibly the current 'go to' method to develop Leaders – and that is a fundamental error in judgment. Without having the proper frameworks, culture, and ethos, conducting Leadership Development Programs has very little impact on the overall development of Leaders. So, before we proceed, it is important to understand that structured Leadership Development Programs must be considered only once the basics and fundamentals (processes, frameworks, and ethos – as discussed in earlier chapters) are in place.

There are some basics you need to factor in and understand unequivocally before you embark on investing in a Leadership development Program – at any level within the organisation:

A. Learning *about* Leadership and *learning to Lead* are two very different things. Learning *about* Leadership is what most Programs offer.
B. Leadership *cannot* be taught (in the typical 'traditional' sense) and needs to be 'learnt.'
C. Learning Leadership Skills requires a *process*-oriented approach to training – not an *event*-based approach.
D. It is important to factor Structured Leadership Development Programs as *part of* a larger Leadership development drive – rather than as a stand-alone Program.
E. Creating such Programs needs to be undertaken *holistically* – where *each level* of development is interconnected to each other – rather than different Programs which are stand-alone for different levels.

The key to remember is this: conducting a 'Leadership development Program' is *not* the objective. The objective ought to be *developing Leaders*. So, the Program is a *part of* that exercise – the Program does *not* become the *exercise* itself. This fundamental difference needs to be understood if Leadership Development Programs are to be effective – and add value to the overall process of developing and growing Leaders.

First, let's put a framework around the Leadership Development Programs – so that there is an inter-connected approach to it.

This illustration on the next page is an amended framework (amended to ensure the exact framework is not shared for confidentiality-related reasons) from one of the biggest private sector organisations in Sri Lanka. The framework illustrates how Leadership development needs to be looked at from a holistic perspective – and will offer insights on how each 'level' will have a connection to the other – and how they need to be interwoven, to ensure there is steady growth in Leadership as Participants go through each stage as part of their structured training initiatives.

A couple of pointers:

- Look at each level of the hierarchy.
- Identify the *core objectives* of *primary focus* for each level. This sets the 'tone' for the Program.
- Notice that aspects like *Values*, the Leadership *Code* and the Competencies are *commonly* taught *across* the hierarchical spaces. This ensures that each level understands what is expected from each level – and enables a better appreciation for the kind of roles each level needs to play in developing Leaders.

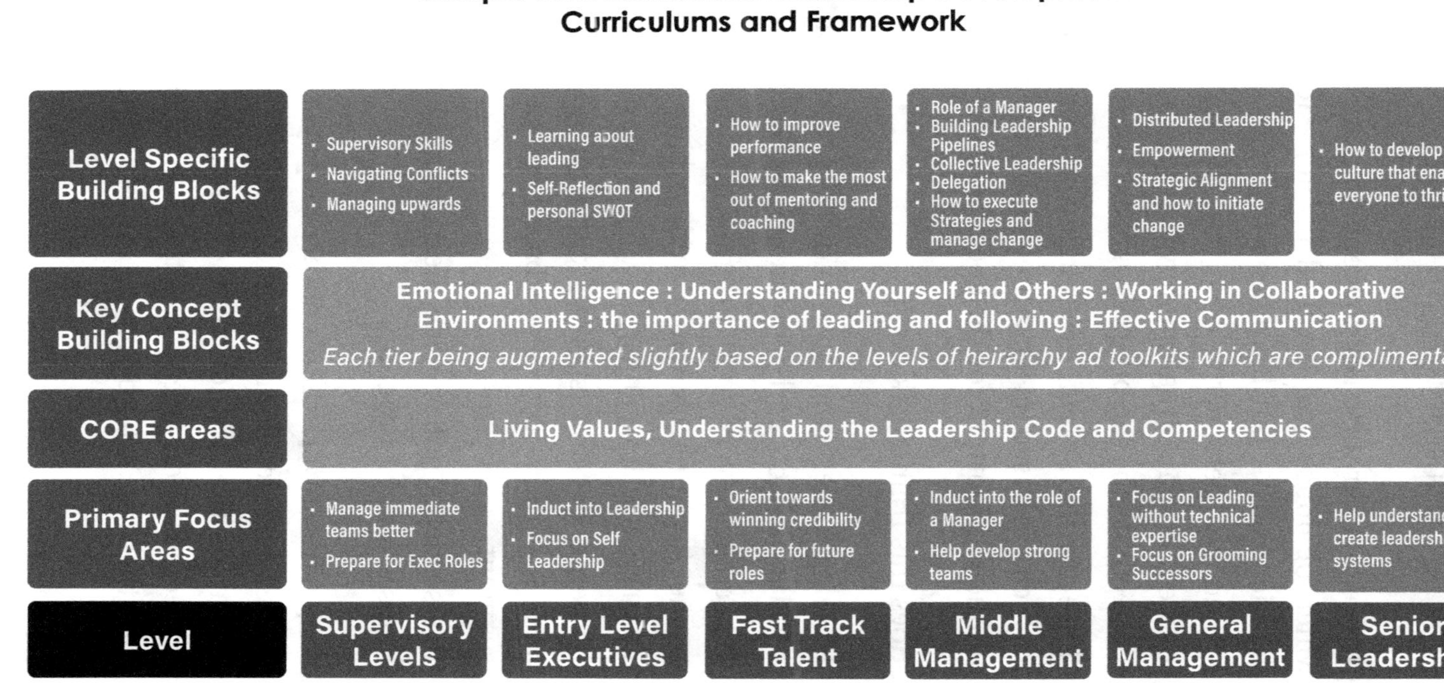
Sample Interconnected Leadership Development
Curriculums and Framework
Level Specific Building Blocks
Supervisory Skills
Navigating Conflicts
Managing upwards
Learning about leading
Self-Reflection and personal SWOT
How to improve performance
How to make the most out of mentoring and coaching
Role of a Manager
Building Leadership Pipelines
Collective Leadership
Delegation
How to execute Strategies and manage change
Distributed Leadership
Empowerment
Strategic Alignment and how to initiate change
How to develop a culture that enables everyone to thrive
Key Concept Building Blocks
Emotional Intelligence : Understanding Yourself and Others : Working in Collaborative Environments : the importance of leading and following : Effective Communication
Each tier being augmented slightly based on the levels of heirarchy ad toolkits which are complimentary
CORE areas
Living Values, Understanding the Leadership Code and Competencies
Primary Focus Areas
Manage immediate teams better
Prepare for Exec Roles
Induct into Leadership
Focus on Self Leadership
Orient towards winning credibility
Prepare for future roles
Induct into the role of a Manager
Help develop strong teams
Focus on Leading without technical expertise
Focus on Grooming Successors
Help understand and create leadership eco systems
Level
Supervisory Levels
Entry Level Executives
Fast Track Talent
Middle Management
General Management
Senior Leadership

- Notice there are also key concepts that are identified, which obviously are 'levelled up' for each level of the hierarchy – but have been kept the same from a 'thematic' perspective – so that the key elements covered in one Program have a relevance and a connectivity for the other Program.
- There are also *specific* areas identified for each level – which are based on what the organisation deems is uniquely important for the specific level.

What does this framework do?

A. It helps understand how to develop common and specific skillsets and competencies at each level.
B. It becomes a very good 'briefing' document for any trainer/training company undertaking to do the Program for the company.
C. It helps develop specific curriculums, toolkits, and principles to teach – based on each specific segment.
D. It also helps put specific measurements/feedback loops around a Program.

So, having a framework of this nature helps you to ensure that Leadership development is looked at holistically – and enables the development of Programs that are interconnected and specific to the organisation. Far too often there is a tendency to simply send selected

Participants to 'standard' Leadership Programs – conducted by various institutes and universities. These are all about *learning about* Leadership (which is certainly useful too) and must not be misunderstood to be *developing Leaders*. Learning *about* Leadership is important – and can be incorporated into some of these segments – but a focused, structured, and tailored set of Leadership Programs needs to be curated, if the organisation is serious about growing Leaders at all levels.

Once you have a framework in place, it is equally important to have a *process* in place for Programs so that it does not end up being an *event*. Most Leadership Development Programs are simply events and nothing more.

Once again – a conceptual framework for *one* of the segments that was identified in the earlier framework. This is the 'process' around the *Executive Development* Program designed *specifically* for the Executive Vertical within the organisation.

Selection of Participants for a Program is crucial. Simply getting a group of Participants together and telling them to go for a 'Leadership Program' is a sure way of doing two things:

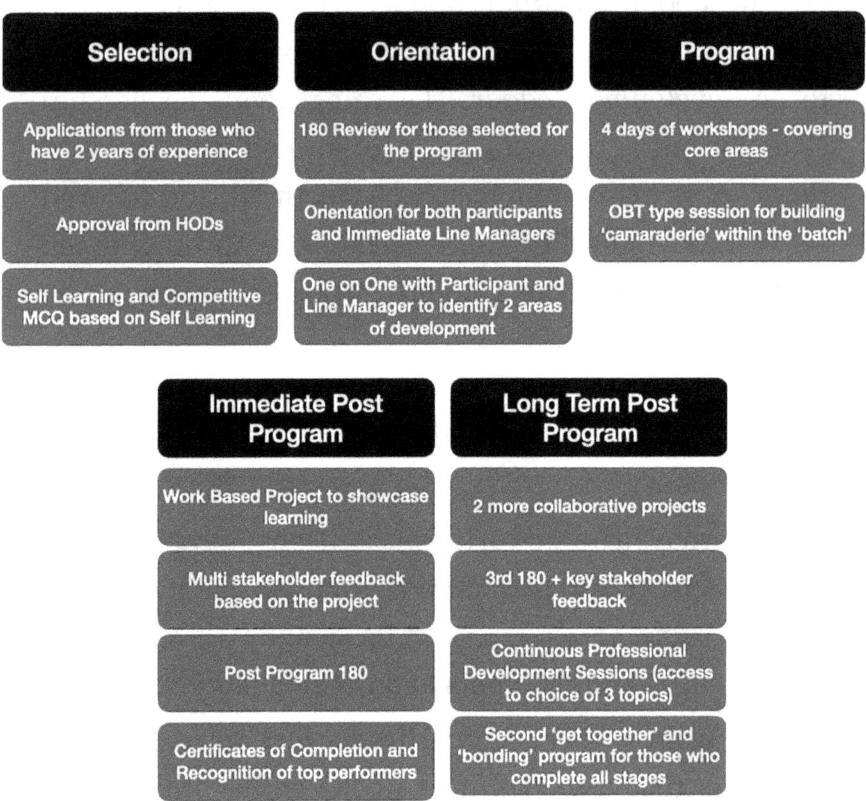

A. Diluting the importance and significance of the Program.

B. Creating an expectation that Leadership training is an 'entitlement' or part of the 'package' within the company.

It is important to ensure that any form of Leadership development Program is something that is 'earned' not simply 'given.' This setting of the tone is critical to ensure there isn't a rather unholy precedence you set – which happens many times over within organisations. I have often heard many 'complain' that 'this year we didn't get any Leadership training' whenever employee opinion surveys have taken place – and I cringe every single time – because this is a clear indication that Leadership training had been diminished to an 'event' – no different to an annual trip, or a Christmas party!

So, when selecting Participants for Leadership Programs, make sure there are set criteria, and selection guidelines. Here is what we do with one of our clients for their EDP Programs:

- *Open the 'nominations' for ALL within the fold – as long as they have completed two years of service within the company (at any level.)*
- *The nomination needs to be 'approved' by the Line Manager. This is a mere formality – if the application is REJECTED, the Line Manager needs to offer explanations for the rejection in writing to HR. The approval process is to ensure that the Line Managers are AWARE of who is applying – nothing more. However, on occasion, Line Managers have rejected applications for sensible reasons – including marriage taking place during the time of the Program workshops, a letter of warning or*

misdemeanour being filed against the Participant, or at times, an overseas visit, etc., being planned during that time.

- *The Participants are then put through a two-month self-learning phase where they are given ten core modules to learn at their own pace. At the end of the first four weeks, we conduct a 'mock and review' process, where we go through the salient points of the self-learning material and conduct a 'mock exam' that orients the Participants to the kind of questions they will have to face. At the end of the stipulated eight weeks, we run the MCQ paper – where 100 questions are asked around the 10 modules given to them.*
- *Getting a pass mark is not enough – because only two batches of thirty Participants each get into the 'workshops' phase – so – you need to be one of the top 60 to get in.*

This process enables a few things to fall into place:

1. No one 'selects' Participants to be 'trained' – the onus of 'development' is now with each individual employee. *If* they are interested in their own development – they are free to apply and come in for the Program.
2. You cannot just 'join' the Program – you need to 'earn your spot' in it. This gives a very, very serious

undertone for the Program – and it also ensures that you have to 'work' towards 'earning your place.'

3. No one can cry 'favouritism' – as it is *your* effort that gets you in. Completing the Program is considered *one* of the criteria for promotion to Assistant Manager levels within the business – so – ensuring you earn your spot is completely in your own hands.
4. This process also ensures that when you come for the workshops *everyone* has their *basic* knowledge in place. Given that the self-learning modules are designed around the 10 topics being covered during the four days of workshops, every Participant can contribute positively towards the conversations.

So, this type of approach ensures that the Participants in the Program not only take the Program seriously, but also come prepared for a much richer conversation and participation.

As much as it is important to focus on selecting the 'right' candidates for a Program, it is important to ensure that the Participants are 'oriented' into the Program – and as importantly – that their Line Managers are also inducted – as they play a crucial role in ensuring the full benefit of the Program is taken from the Program by the Participants.

The induction and orientation for the Program are done in two phases.

First, there is a launch. The launch involves a series of Presentations, including a Senior Manager who talks about the importance of the Program, and why this investment is being made, a Presentation from HR about the expectations from both the Participants AND their Line Managers, and a Presentation from the Learning Facilitators about the Program flow and logistics. ALL dates are sent in advance for ALL workshops AND other interventions – and those dates are blocked out and approved by the Senior Leadership – and express instructions given to Line Managers that the Participants need to be released at all costs.

Second, there is a one-on-one that takes place based on 180 or 360 feedback. The Learning Facilitator guides a conversation with the Participants and their respective Line Managers and hones in on identifying 1-2 key areas for development for the INDIVIDUAL, which becomes what each individual Participant puts a Personal Development Plan around, as part of the Program. This one-on-one also features a conversation with the Line Manager about SPECIFIC interventions they need to perform in order to ensure the learning outcomes are achieved. This process ensures each Line Manager becomes an active stakeholder in the Leadership development process.

The selection process and the orientation process ensure that both the Participants and the key Line Managers are active Participants in the development of Leadership in the Participants. This is critical given that *after* the workshops are done, Participants are expected to conduct a Project which is assessed for effectiveness and impact, and linked to the development objectives identified in the 360/180 one-on-ones. So, without the Line Managers being 'involved' in the 'process' the post-program interventions cannot be implemented effectively.

The workshops are designed to teach tools and techniques to cover identified competencies. The curriculums need to vary to ensure the required competencies are given focus. However, it is important to ensure:

- Tools are a specific focus – not just concepts.
- Ensure tools are appropriate to the context of the organisation.
- There is *time* to actually *try out* the tools during the workshops themselves – and assess their validity.
- Peer Review processes are in-built and encouraged – and wide-open conversations about the application of the tools and concepts are built in, to ensure what is taught is understood to be 'practical' rather than 'theoretical.'
- There is a time accorded, for reflection and internalisation – and to ensure that specific applications can be addressed

On the following page is an illustration of how this 'design process' of a Program is done – with 'Making collective decisions' being the focus area:

Sample Design of a Specific Program

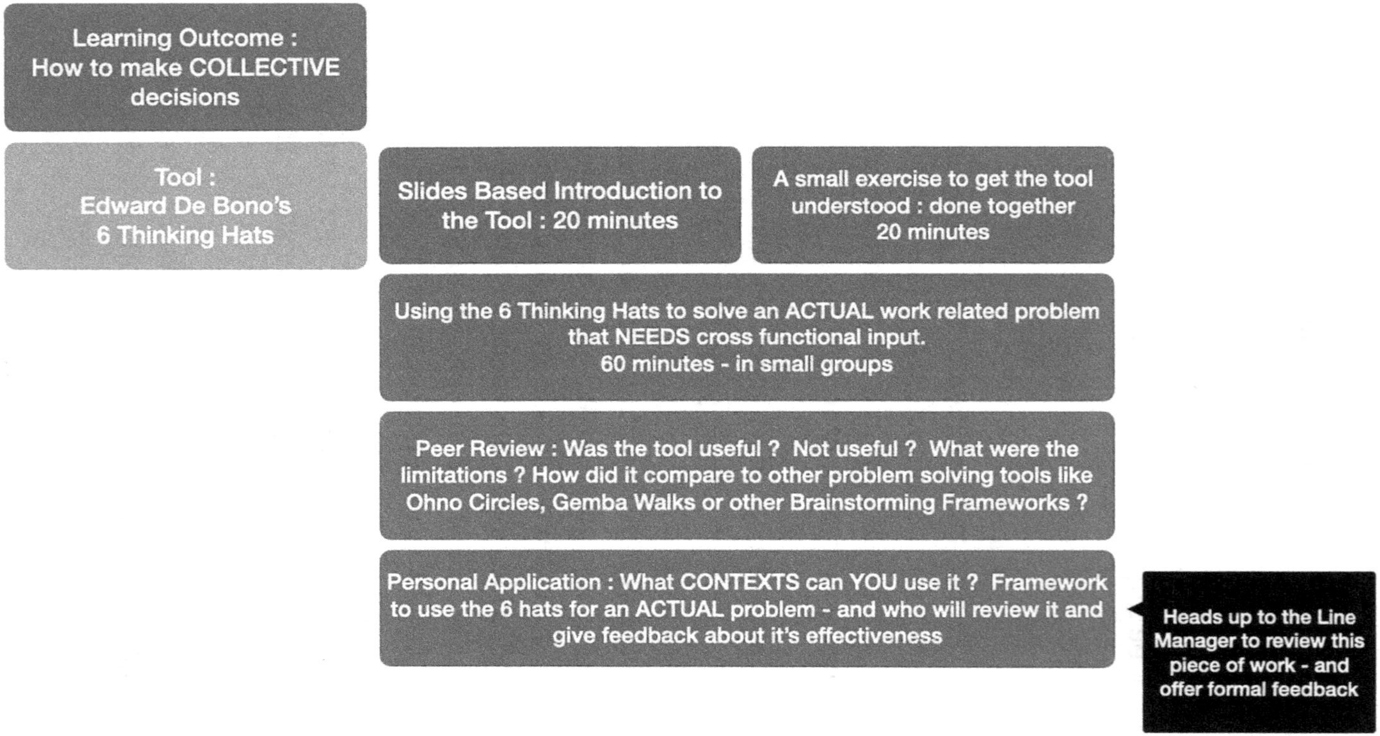

Learning Outcome :
How to make COLLECTIVE decisions

Tool :
Edward De Bono's
6 Thinking Hats

Slides Based Introduction to the Tool : 20 minutes

A small exercise to get the tool understood : done together
20 minutes

Using the 6 Thinking Hats to solve an ACTUAL work related problem that NEEDS cross functional input.
60 minutes - in small groups

Peer Review : Was the tool useful ? Not useful ? What were the limitations ? How did it compare to other problem solving tools like Ohno Circles, Gemba Walks or other Brainstorming Frameworks ?

Personal Application : What CONTEXTS can YOU use it ? Framework to use the 6 hats for an ACTUAL problem - and who will review it and give feedback about it's effectiveness

Heads up to the Line Manager to review this piece of work - and offer formal feedback

Leadership Development Programs need to be different to other 'training' Programs – in that – there needs to be a definitive design focus on ensuring a tool is taught – applied in the 'learning space' as well as ensuring there is a loop to see if the tool can be applied in *work settings* and then, internalised as part of the toolkit the Participant uses on a regular basis. Unless this cyclical process happens, and is piggybacked into reflections, there isn't *real* learning – there is only an amassing of 'knowledge' which you leave to chance to become 'applied skills.'

Leadership Development Programs MUST bridge this gap – otherwise, there is no REAL benefit from the Program. The DIFFERENCE between a 'seminar' or a 'workshop' on Leadership and a Leadership Development Program is fundamentally this – that in a Leadership Development Program Participants must not only learn concepts and tools – but they must be able to practice them – accept that they can be applied in their 'real world' and then, be able to actually DO IT in their own work contexts AND be reviewed for it. This PROCESS is what defines Leadership development – NOT the 'workshop' itself per se.

So, any Program must ensure there is a solid process around it that ensures APPLIED SKILLS are developed – NOT simply KNOWLEDGE.

This overall appreciation for the end objective of developing Leaders – rather than simply 'teaching about Leadership' – is important to be put into the structure

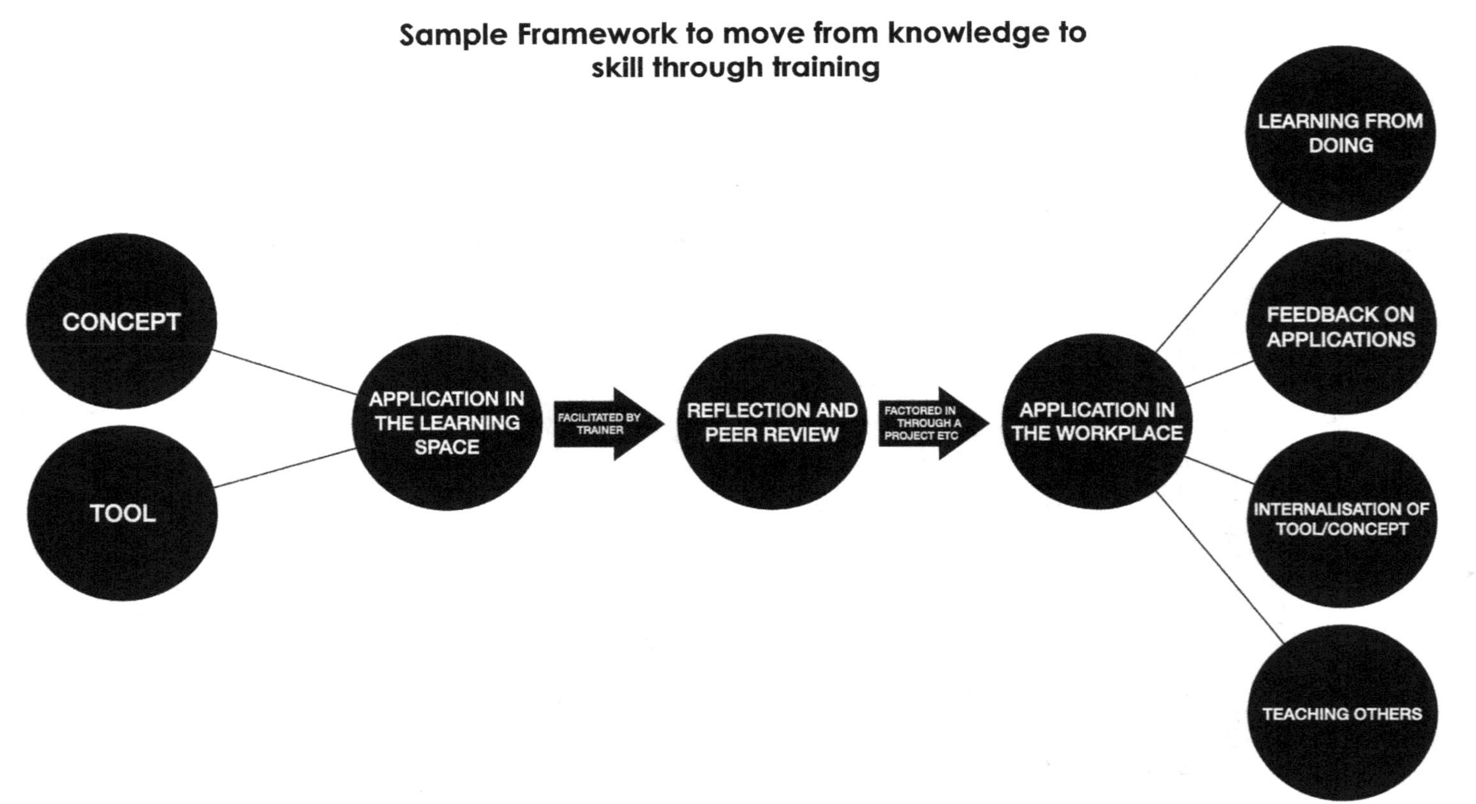
Sample Framework to move from knowledge to skill through training
CONCEPT
TOOL
APPLICATION IN THE LEARNING SPACE
FACILITATED BY TRAINER
REFLECTION AND PEER REVIEW
FACTORED IN THROUGH A PROJECT ETC
APPLICATION IN THE WORKPLACE
LEARNING FROM DOING
FEEDBACK ON APPLICATIONS
INTERNALISATION OF TOOL/CONCEPT
TEACHING OTHERS

and design of any level of Leadership development intervention.

Generally, nothing much happens *after* a training Program apart from feedback about the Program from Participants. So, ensuring there is a solid set of activities *after* the Program that is aligned to assessing learning and capability enhancement and application of the learning is important.

The EDP process identified above has several interventions to ensure that:

A. *Learning Application is assessed.*
B. *Capability enhancement is assessed.*
C. *Ability to bring in RESULTS through learning application is assessed.*

The way this is done is by giving each Participant the opportunity to do a work-based Project:

- *The Project needs to be outside their job scope. This forces them to use 'influence' rather than 'authority' to get things done. It also offers the additional benefit of enabling your emergent Leaders to understand a process/area in the business that they may not always work with – thus expanding their appreciation for the wider business.*

- *The Project needs to be 'completed' in 8 weeks. This forces Participants to scope something reasonable – and actionable. It also ensures they have a definitive timeline set, to ensure their progress.*
- *The Project needs to have a QUANTIFIABLE result. This forces the Participants to look at how to make DEFINITIVE IMPACT not merely make recommendations.*
- *The Project needs to be approved by the HOD of the 'beneficiary' department – this forces Participants to 'sell' their idea to a different Unit Head – outside of their own Line Manager. It also forces Line Managers to be open to being critiqued by 'outsiders', enabling a more open culture overall.*

Notice that the 'Project' is NOT simply 'finding fault' and 'making recommendations.' It is a piece of work where Participants need to commit time, energy, and effort to ensure they SOLVE a problem AND bring in a RESULT.

After the Project is completed, the following takes place:

- *A Report submitted – signed off by the 'beneficiary department' confirming the results. The Report has an entire section on how the 'learning was applied.'*
- *A Presentation is made to the external trainer/ assessor, HR and Line Manager – and learning outcomes as well as overall results from the Project analysed and formerly assessed.*

- *360-based Reviews of the key learning outcomes being applied and practised are assessed – and shared with the Line Manager and Participant during the assessment. This includes work done on the individual development area identified during the initial one-on-one discussion.*

Only those who complete the Project phase are given the Certificate of Completion.

Furthermore, the following activities are actioned out after the certificates are offered to continue the learning journey:

- *Two more Projects are undertaken – this time in small groups rather than individually. Freedom is given for these to be done in any section of the business – but subject to the same conditions listed for the individual Project.*
- *Projects are assessed using the same criteria – and once again, learning is measured and given feedback. 360s are used to assess behaviours during the Projects from stakeholders. This feedback too is offered as part of the assessment.*
- *Continuous Professional Development 'forums' are organised. This particular client has 24 sessions – two per month being done on designated dates. Those who have completed the individual Projects can come for three of the sessions of their choosing.*

- *Those who complete all these phases are given a 'special' Program where they have training combined with a 'get together' of the 'batch' and are given a weekend stay along with it. This brings the entire process to a close. A final 180/360 is generally done as a closing Review.*

Notice that the evaluation process is also not a one-off event. It is a series of interventions – each as a buildup of the other. Learning is reflected upon, put into practice, made use of to bring in a tangible result to the business *and* reviewed and feedback is offered from multiple stakeholder perspectives. This robust process enables the Program to carefully 'distil' those who grow with learning – and those who don't really make use of the opportunities to learn. It also offers the opportunity for the entire senior Leadership to assess, in a very unbiased way, the potential the candidates have for further advancement within the organisation. For Participants, it offers a wonderful opportunity to showcase their talents to the wider organisation.

The Leadership Development Training Framework adopted by the Knit Cluster of the Hirdaramani Group is an illustrative example of this entire framework being put into practice. The organisation has an integrated Leadership competency framework and a Leadership code that acts as the backbone for all Leadership development work – and ALL the training Programs at every level are linked DIRECTLY to the Competencies and the Code. Each layer has a distinctive Program – including two 'bridge' Programs for 'top talent' and those who are 'fast-tracked' from non-executive grades into the executive grades. The Programs are all interlinked. All supervisory levels are conducted by internal trainers – and all executive level upwards are conducted by external trainers including international training institutions such as the Centre for Creative Leadership taking some aspects of the Programs. However, no matter who conducts the Programs, the assessment frameworks are managed internally and mapped every step of the way – with a 'learning leaderboard' maintained.

There is also a DIRECT link to the 9-box framework – and this in turn is DIRECTLY linked to the career advancement framework. The ENTIRE development framework is 'connected' end to end – with clear assessment methodologies at each step. The Leadership Development Programs are ONE PART of the process – and are DIRECTLY interlinked to the wider framework, which is what makes it so effective.

Quite apart from the assessment of learning outcomes, Hirdaramani also calculates DIRECT ROI after Leadership training and records an impressive three times ROI on average for the past ten years – INCLUDING the Covid years. This is one of the reasons why the training budget has never been slashed for the past decade – because Leadership training is definitively considered an INVESTMENT not a COST.

Chapter 10

Peer Learning in Growing Leaders

"Most of us who are not on the brilliant side of the spectrum learn more from our fellow students than from our teachers..."

Possibly one of the least celebrated and most underrated development methodologies for growing Leaders is that of Peer Learning initiatives and frameworks. It is worthwhile to factor this in as a fundamental design element in the development framework for Leadership, because there is enough credible merit to prove that we learn as much (if not more) from our peers as much as from our superiors, and through other training/coaching/development interventions.

The challenge however is this: Most peer-level learning around Leadership-related aspects happens 'by chance' and as part of 'unconscious learning' by observation, conversations, working together and assimilation. It is almost never done 'consciously' and within any form of formalised process or framework.

The case for Peer Learning is simple. Think of the time when you were in school – and you could not really 'get it.' Who did you REALLY learn from? Did you ask your teacher to explain it five times over until you 'got it' – or did you reach out to one of your fellow students and sit down with them to understand how to work the sum? Think of a meeting where something critical was being discussed – and you were not quite sure of the contexts, discussion points OR final outcomes. It was all a little 'blur' for you. Do you go to your boss – or the convener of the meeting – and tell them to explain it all to you so that you 'get it' – or would you reach out to a colleague? Imagine a tough situation you had to deal with as a first-time Manager – in which you may have to consider taking serious disciplinary action against someone within the Team – whom would you feel most comfortable talking to – your superiors – or a peer Manager who got promoted with you?

Peers play an integral role in our development as Leaders. However, just like learning by 'mimicking' our superiors, learning from peers is a double-edged sword. You can learn the good – the bad – and the ugly from them, and unless this is rationalised and managed, what you 'learn' is down to the peers you keep company with most.

The bottom line is this. We *do* learn from our peers. We also compare and contrast our actions with our peers – and they become a 'standard' of measurement to assess our behavioursa against. Being able to put a small structure around Peer Learning helps organisations take control of this 'unconscious learning' and put some semblance of control over it – in a positive way. Be warned – one can *never* fully formalise this – nor should you – learning happens, anyway. *But*, to ensure you learn what you *need* to learn, having a small framework certainly helps.

Peers can play both Mentor and Coach roles. However, rather than looking at it from an either/or perspective, the best way for peer-level learning to take place is in the form of encouraging structures around already existing relationships, friendships and 'cliques' which happen without any structure or formality around it. It is common for workplace friendships to forge – for 'cliques' of friends to go out together – and for many of these relationships remain and grow, as they grow in their careers. So, rather than 'forcing' learning, the idea is to 'enable' learning from each other in a more structured way – benefiting all parties concerned.

A word of caution before we proceed with modalities. Peers are also where rivalries are the deepest. Peer rivalries for the limited senior positions tend to create power struggles and a tug-of-war effect that often can rip through structures and cause great divisions in Teams. So, be mindful of the 'flip side' when creating Peer Learning Frameworks. If done carefully and wisely, these Peer Learning frameworks can also act to mitigate some of the negatives stemming from peer-level rivalries –

Peers as Friends and Rivals

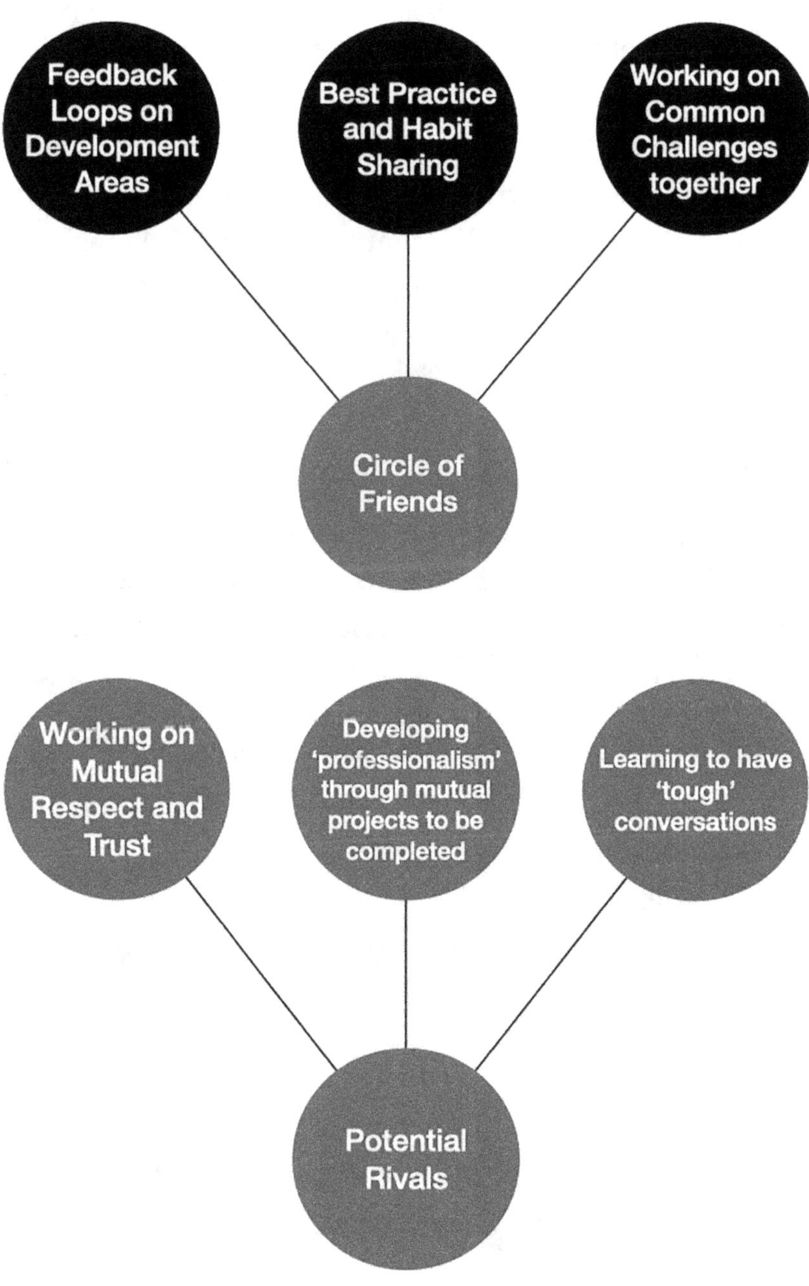

and enable some mutual respect and trust between even 'warring' peers.

Some of the key lessons learnt through various organisations with regards to simple practices that showcase how effective Peer Learning frameworks can be are summarised in this chapter, to give some insights into how you can benefit from such schemes too – as summarised and illustrated, above.

First, let us look at how we can make use of Circles of Friends to help develop Leadership competencies and skills. Peers who become Circles of Friends become a brilliant network to:

- Give honest, candid, and straightforward feedback.
- Share best practices and tips/hacks/insights on how to do things better – both as a Manager and as a Leader.
- Become cross-functional Teams that work on improvement Projects of common interest/focus.

Sometimes, all three of these aspects can be covered through a well-crafted Project that they undertake. Here is an example from GSK Sri Lanka in the early 2000s.

In an attempt to ensure the Leaders within Sales

Teams were developed – and worked TOGETHER towards a push to ensure the sales revenue was doubled within five years (GSK at the time was a 1Bn in sales revenue – which took the business nearly 50 years to achieve – and the challenge was to make it 2Bn in just five years) the Senior Leadership Team came up with a rather 'unique' solution to crunching the learning curve. Rather than over-relying on traditional training and development processes (which DID take place through the GSK Academy), they looked at 'cliques' of colleagues, and organised them into small 'Teams' who were to 'help each other' better drive their own respective Teams. The growth objectives were very aggressive, where the business had to grow at a Compound Annual Growth Rate (CAGR) of 16% YOY in a market that was growing at a single digit rate.

- *They were encouraged to meet often – some of their meetings were 'funded' by their immediate superiors.*
- *They discussed their common challenges.*
- *They swapped Sales Representatives between them – to give them territories or products that better suited their skills.*
- *They shared best practices – and also – tried out certain common initiatives – such as pooling resources to attract key 'doctors' who held sway for the big-ticket items.*

They also did something very, very instrumental in developing each other: they started giving each other candid feedback based on their own observations. Generally done over a beer on a Friday, these 'heart to heart' sessions were often brutal in their critique of each other – but no one took offence because they knew each other well enough – and were friends for some time. These feedback sessions were never disclosed to anyone else apart from themselves – and at times – some got very heated, too. However, outside of HR and Corporate influences and framing or observation, they were self-regulated and were never destructive.

Many who were part of this exercise tell us that these were possibly the most 'brutal' critiques of their behaviours and capabilities that they have ever had in their entire career thus far. Rather than simply 'criticising' they discussed what to do about it, too – and knowing full well they would be 'called out' if they 'committed' to improvement and if they then did not follow through with action, all those involved were sincere in their undertakings of areas for improvement. These 'heart to heart' sessions helped develop Leadership skills – and drove their sales performances up.

The Team DID achieve the 2Bn mark in five years – and in fact, bettered that too – to become 3Bn in three years! The brands they built are market Leaders even today.

As much as friends, 'rivals' can be a great source of development as well. Though needless to say, initiatives involving 'rivals' need to be implemented with a lot more care and sensitivity, they are, nonetheless, a great opportunity to build Leadership capabilities and potential.

Another extreme example. This one is from a past life as a young Assistant Manager. I had just been promoted to Assistant Manager HRD and was in charge of all Learning and Development initiatives. I was ambitious, driven, and, extremely buoyant about what I wanted to implement within the business. The company was keen to ensure they had a clear differentiation based on Quality and Quality Management, and our Managing Director brought in Piyal Aponso as the Manager Quality to spearhead the initiative and transformation.

Piyal was possibly THE most qualified person we had within the business – holding a Bachelors degree from the University of Sri Jayewardenepura (the University with the Premier Management Faculty on the island) and a MBA from the Post Graduate Institute of Management. He was also certified as an ISO Auditor, and held numerous other certifications and accolades. In fact, he was one of only TWO in the entire business with a Masters level qualification. He was also well experienced – with over fifteen years of hands-on quality management experience and expertise. He came in and started steering the company towards ISO certification with the zeal of a missionary and the enthusiasm of a starving boy at a buffet!

Sadly, he and I got off on the wrong foot – and very soon we were at loggerheads. His rather 'strait-jacketed' approach to Quality and 'Process' did not sit well with me – and I took offence at his 'meddling' with 'my affairs' in MY department. The fact that he had to put 'procedures' in 'all departments' in order to ensure there was a systematic approach to 'quality' was lost on me – and I looked at his 'intrusions' into 'my territory' as a sign of a personal attack on me and my management style.

Things got really bad – and it was impacting the overall deadline of the ISO certification as well. Our Managing Director's approach to us 'settling our scores' is a story for another time – but – having sorted it out in the short term – he initiated a small 'plan' to ensure Piyal and I (and a few others who were not really 'toeing the line together') were able to learn from each other and develop a healthy mutual respect for each other. We learnt about his 'trick' only much later – when both of us were Senior Managers. Fate played a part in this, as this occurred on the day I submitted my resignation, and told my MD that I was ready to move on from the company.

Shirendra, our MD, sent Piyal and me alone to a sister company with the instruction to ensure we do an audit together and understand their key lag points – and to come back with several best practices the unit was known for. He got the both of us to travel together – stay in the same 'apartment' together – and work on the assignment for two whole weeks before coming back. He told me to give my feedback about Piyal – and told Piyal to give him feedback about me (which neither of us knew till we came back). I was livid that I had to do this with Piyal – as was he – but, knowing that we had too much to lose and that our MD was not one to take things lightly if we came back with half-baked Reports, we were forced to work with each other.

The structure for the assignment was regimentalised by our MD. We had Reports to fill in each day – formats to follow and also, Project plans to be done BEFORE we came back. So, each night, after we had come from the plant visits and meetings, we would sit down and work – and compare each other's notes – put it together – and make 'game plans' for implementation of best practices once we got back to CCL. Working together – away from the usual hubbub of operational activity – it was plain to see that Piyal was very, very competent – and that he 'knew what he was talking about' and that his focus was clearly on ensuring we have process-driven quality management systems that cut across the entire business – rather than the narrow focus on 'quality assurance' which we were used to. At the same time, Piyal understood that my 'creative' and often 'non-conformist' approaches to HR and HRD had their positives – and carried with them the possibility to help him embed quality as a way of life – rather than simply a function or a department.

By the time we came back – we were still not friends – but we were certainly not 'enemies' either – and we had gained a certain healthy respect for each other.

Shirendra followed this up with three other key initiatives:

- *Joint Project – where we had to implement best practices together – pegged to 30% of our overall KPI score.*
- *A Peer Review of each other, monthly.*
- *Piyal to teach me quality management – and for me to teach him HRD-related aspects.*

He made the two of us 'Review' each other regularly – and the first Performance Review was one that he took with him being present. He told me to review my perspectives of Piyal based on our values and also certain 'competencies' that were listed out – and Piyal did the same for me. It was utterly awkward and extremely uncomfortable for the both of us – but – we had to do it. Once this was done, Shirendra asked us to do it regularly – and to submit 'Reports' on the same. These 'conversations' were awkward for nearly four or five sessions, but at some point, turned into genuine conversations about each other's strengths and weaknesses, and over time, spilt over into awareness of how we can help each other, on a continuing basis. We ended up giving 'joint Reports' to our MD – and, by that time, we all knew that there was no need for formalities.

Some key achievements:

A. *We completed ISO 90001, 14001 AND Social Compliance Certifications (2 of them) all in the same year. This could never have been possible if Piyal and I did not work together.*
B. *We developed an ongoing training plan on quality – ensuring that everyone within the company was 'inducted' into the 'quality way of life' – enabling us to implement quality management systems and statistical process control mechanisms – and not increase the 'quality controller' role as we grew our headcount.*
C. *We also incorporated the Quality Management Process approach to all training we did – which is actually where the inspiration for 'process oriented' approach to 'Leadership development' also saw birth!*
D. *We were identified as one of the best plants for quality and related management practices – as well as HRD practices – and we were able to win several big-ticket awards over the next two years, including the Inaugural National HR Award (First Runner Up – and being the ONLY garment manufacturer to win an award that year) – to all of which achievements Piyal had offered much-needed weight and impetus.*

We STILL remain friends...

One of the other 'fringe benefits' of this was that the rest of the Management Team saw us working together – and used us as an 'example' to look at how 'petty rivalries' can be put aside. Often when colleagues had rivalries, Piyal and I would instinctively step in – and help them, wherever possible.

Being able to bring 'rivals' together – in the spirit of not just teamwork or collaboration – but in the spirit of *learning Leadership* is important. Generally, warring peers are brought together because of the need for teamwork – which is a must for sure – but – use these opportunities to enable them to *learn Leadership*, too. Being able to set aside differences and work towards a common objective – and being able to let go of your ego towards something greater than yourself is essential in Leadership, and an absolute must if you want to grow as a Leader. Peer rivalries are great opportunities to offer the space to learn just that – provided you are willing to wade carefully, and make sure you are able to see through it. Once again, what is important is that there is a definitive framework (formal or informal) around it – and also – that it is supported and seen through. These must not be undertaken lightly – nor should they be considered 'initiatives' as such – they must become ongoing activities that are undertaken as and when the situation lets itself positively towards it.

Apart from creating structured frameworks towards Peer Learning, it is important to 'facilitate' the Peer Learning process that happens nearly automatically. Many times, we see organisations having little initiatives that lend themselves quite nicely towards the propagation and encouragement of Peer Learning across the organisational setting.

Here are some samples to offer some insights and help look at introducing some Peer Learning opportunities within an organisational fold.

1. *The 'Buddy System' has gained considerable popularity within the garment manufacturers in Sri Lanka. One of the biggest challenges within a factory is attrition within the first six months – especially due to production-related pressures. So, the newcomers are given a 'buddy' to 'look after' them and also, act as their mentor and Coach for the first six months. After the completion of their probation, the 'buddy' remains for a further six months, and are often given another 'fresher' if they are successful with the first set. The 'buddy' is often someone earmarked for promotion to a Supervisory category. This is considered one of their 'assessments' and 'training' opportunities. Working with and on behalf of those coming in new, the 'buddy' learns to empathise with newcomers, understand their issues, resolve what they can, and*

act on their behalf, all of which becomes invaluable when they get promoted to a Line Leader or Supervisor role.

2. *'Ask a Friend' is a scheme which we observed in a small-scale facility which was producing dehydrated fruits. With a shortage of skilled staff and not being able to cope with increased demand and related growth, the owner of the business initiated a scheme called 'call a friend' where the operators can resolve a problem by literally 'calling a friend' within the company and asking for their advice. There was a small log book to put an entry on what the problem was, what the solution was, that was given, and also, what the result was. At the end of each month, the owner offered some form of financial and at times non-financial incentive to those who had helped others, and also shared the 'best solutions' with the entire (factory) floor. This institutionalised a form of knowledge sharing amongst peers and also encouraged developing a certain openness between different sections of the business which were usually not working together. It was clear that there were plenty of people in different departments who COULD help. The 'log book' became a 'reference' to find out who to seek out. (This was an SME business – and the idea of 'logging' problems and solutions was picked up by an IT company, which developed an elaborate*

system to log problems and solutions and thereby created a repository of tacit knowledge.)

3. *A really interesting and novel idea we observed in India was the weekly 'debates' which were institutionalised in a medium-scale retail company. The scheme was simple. Each week, the BIGGEST issues/policy-related aspects that the organisation/ Team faced were 'debated' to find solutions and insights. Topics ranging from 'Should Performance be Linked to Pay?' To 'Should Customer be Treated Like a King?' were debated, and audiences were given the opportunity to give in their perspectives. This was institutionalised for any major policy decision – where the entire organisation (of around 150 people) came together, listened to the debate, gave their insights; and only then were the decisions made. How does this help Leadership development? First, those who WANTED policy changes had to 'debate it out' with others – and second, it makes any decision completely transparent – a tough lesson to learn in Leadership. How does this become 'Peer Learning'? In this instance, the organisation was very flat, so this kind of intervention took the 'hierarchy' out of the equation, bringing a lot more focus on merit. This enabled 'Peer Learning' because it forces peers to listen to each other – talk it out – and also, put themselves out to scrutiny in front of the entire organisation.*

4. *A superb illustration of Peer Learning at Senior Levels of Leadership was a scheme we observed in the Middle East at a relatively large financial services sector organisation. Here, where the Senior Team was made up of over 15 nationalities from across the globe, the Head of HR initiated a forum to pair Senior Managers monthly to 'TEACH ONE THING TO ME.' The 'pair' worked very closely for the month - and actually were allowed to 'move' their seating if it helped, too. In this month, the duo would share one major competency, skill, technical aspect, 'hack' etc. with the other – and they would also observe them practice it – and give feedback on it. Every week the pairs changed, until they had all met at least 50% of their core Team. Whilst creating amazing friendships and bonds, the scheme also enabled the sharing of global best practices and insights. It also helped build Leadership capability across the board with the added bonus of helping create a solid 'Leadership Team.'*
5. *An exceptionally daring scheme of Peer Learning was the 'Call Me Out' initiative that was initiated by one of the units of a Sri Lankan conglomerate. The scheme was simple – after implementing their new Values and Leadership Competencies, each Senior Manager was given three colleagues who were charged with 'Calling Them Out' if they did not live by the Values/Competencies. This could be done in public – or privately (though almost*

all 'calling outs' were privately done), and they had to do it within 24 hours of observing the non-conformist behaviour. This created a huge focus on observing one's own behaviours – and given that it was a close peer that was 'calling them out' they had much more honest and often 'jovial' conversations around it – rather than it being a 'finger pointing' exercise.

Peers play a huge role in the development of Leadership skills and competencies – and they can equally impede it. If you want to grow Leaders across the organisation, each layer of peers needs to be given the opportunity to help in the development of their colleagues. Having formal frameworks helps, and it also helps to create spaces and initiatives that foster the informal development process, to make it more robust and impactful. Whether it is done formally or informally – structured or unstructured – what is critical is to understand and acknowledge the role peers *do* play in the development process – and, as much as possible, to facilitate it.

Chapter 11

Encouraging Self Reflection and Introspection – and the Role of Self Learning and Self Development

"Without introspection, there is no conscious learning."

Leadership Development within organisations is almost always seen as something HR or the Organisation must do *for* the individual concerned, which is a misnomer, in that ultimately, only *you* can *truly* learn to be a Leader. For sure, the organisation needs to create the right environment and ecosystem in which you can thrive – but, ultimately, after all that is said and done, the onus *ought* to be with *you*. Why? Well... because you can take a horse to water...

So, before anything else, you must create the *need* in the Employees to *want to become Leaders*. After all, why waste your time, energy, and resources on those who do not want to grow themselves, and do not make the commitment to do so?

We took a small preamble to this in *Chapter 8* when we discussed the role of Self Learning as a 'filter' to select Participants for structured Leadership Development Training Programs. The principle was exactly this: to discern between those who wanted to commit to their own development *before* they were invested in (the form of training.) There is a much bigger role self-learning can play in Leadership development; and it is also fundamental that this is done – because – as discussed earlier – only the individual can truly learn to lead. No one else can do it for them.

There are many avenues of self-learning – and what is highlighted above are some critical considerations for an individual for the purpose of developing as a Leader. Notice that it is important to *want* to learn and develop – and also, equally important is an organisational culture/ framework/impetus to enable an individual or influence an individual to improve their Leadership skills, too. One without the other honestly is counterproductive.

Ultimately, each individual needs to become a lifelong student if they are to truly develop themselves as Leaders. Leadership is a journey – it is not a destination. At different stages of your career, at different stages of the organisation's growth curve and in different contexts and situations, how *you* need to contribute as a Leader varies significantly. The *biggest* challenge in developing Leaders

Sample Self Learning Framework

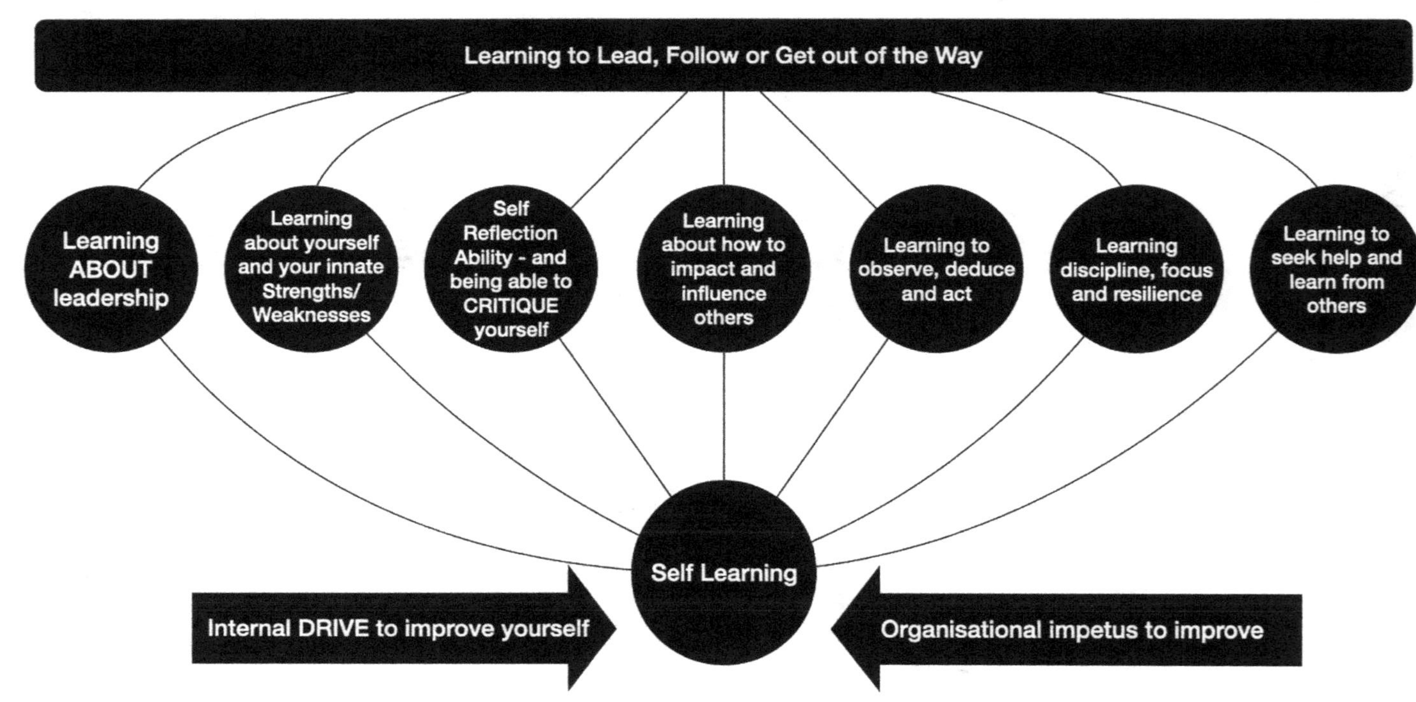

is a myth based on the fact that it is strongly believed that there is 'one best way to lead', which blindsides many organisations not to look at Leadership as an evolving, contextual, and situational role – and *not* a permanent role *or* a permanent set of 'preferred' behaviours.

The *fundamental* requirement of self-learning is this: you need to learn to *lead, follow* or *get out of the way*. Lead, when required, Follow, when required and know when to get out of the way without being a roadblock or impediment to others or the organisations when you can't do both. Leaders *cannot* and *must not* get in the way of success – that is not Leadership – that is merely ego – which is the antecedent of good Leadership. So, the primary objective of self-learning and self-development is to be able to discern when to lead, when to follow, and when to *not* be the problem, and get out of the way.

The first facet of self-learning is to become a lifelong student of Leadership. Leadership is a vast subject area and *learning about* Leadership is important in its own right. Any *good* student is first taught that there is *no one definition* for anything – and being able to discern between the value of each definition, framework, and theory based on its applicability and context is a core component of learning Leadership. Being able to appreciate the different theories, concepts, ideologies, and tools, and appreciate each one as a 'student' of the 'subject', offers the practitioner a rich appreciation for Leadership. This continuous seeking of knowledge about leading and Leadership also gives the practitioner the ability to 'try out' things far more than someone who merely learns from experience. They will also be able to understand frameworks and 'patterns' when they see certain situations - all of which help them become a better Leader.

How can you encourage the 'learning about Leadership' within organisational settings? One of the simplest ways was something one of my former bosses and Mentors Steve Jesseph used to do for me. Every month, Steve sends me a small set of articles (and often books he has read.) I could see that he himself has read all that he sends me, because they are highlighted, commented on and oftentimes present themselves with little 'post its' on them, with ideas and suggestions. He does not expect me to read ALL of it all at the same time – but the fact that he would casually start a conversation about an article or a chapter off a book quickly made me realise that I AM expected to read what he sent me. This became a habit – and has continued to this date – and it is something I too adopted doing with my own Teams, since.

A more structured and framework-based approach to this was observed with one of our clients – who has a weekly set of articles from HBR, McKinsey and also, book chapters from books such as Good to Great being posted on a shared drive. At each weekly meeting, each

Team takes five minutes to give a quick summary based on one article or document. Given that this happens weekly, and everyone is in attendance, it has created a forum to discuss thoughts – and also – reflect on some counter points which invariably get raised. Something we observed with quite a lot of interest is that many who share the learnings related the 'theory' or the 'tool' to a practical event or situation that happened in the workplace, and spoke about how this particular concept or tool was seen being applied (or not applied, and, therefore, the 'issue' still being there) and what could be learnt from it.

A more extreme example was seen with another client of ours who makes it mandatory for all in their Teams to do two 'self-learning sessions' prescribed for them in their LMS (mostly from LinkedIn and other such platforms) per month as part of their Continuous Professional Development KPI. The sessions are tracked, and also, each session has a corresponding 'test' that leads to a small 'certificate.' Each is on a different aspect of Leadership or a related topic. Each year, unless you have 24 duly completed Programs, the Employees are not given the opportunity to be considered for future promotions.

Another big part of self-learning and self-development is the ability to Learn about *yourself* and be able to *self reflect* about your own strengths and weaknesses, and what to do about them. This self-reflection and introspection are both a skill that needs to be developed and a habit that needs to be formed, if you are really interested in growing as a Leader. This self-awareness is the cornerstone of any development of yourself.

Where do you start? We are certainly capable of self-reflection – but how do you LEARN how to do this? A great example of institutionalising self-reflection and growth thereof in a systematic and structured approach is something that was introduced by one of our friends who herself is a consultant and Leadership trainer. Mihirini De Soyza is a much sought-after personal Coach for key Seniors in Sri Lanka's top Corporates. With a PhD from the Ashridge Business School in the UK, and being a Certified Professional Coach, Mihirini helps Senior Leaders develop the ability and the skill to self-reflect – and her go-to 'tool' is that of journaling. Incorporating many tools and techniques from her various areas of academic and professional study, Mihirini gets Senior Leaders to chronicle key incidents and situations and using a journal, dissect the key Leadership lessons they ought to learn from it. Many make this a practice long after her coaching assignment has been concluded, and one told us that he was so 'hooked' on the method and the results he has seen from it that he 'institutionalised' it at home with his kids – telling us that he sees a 'marked difference' in how 'my son and daughter deal with situations after they started journaling on self-reflection.'

Teaching young Leaders, the importance of self-reflection early on is hugely beneficial. You may need to 'train' people on it – but what is critical is to have this become part and parcel of their own development and growth.

Borrowing from Mihirini's approach, here is an idea we mooted with one of our key Clients. Consider the idea of giving each of your Team members a book with 6 sections in it.

A. Success Stories
B. Failure Stories
C. Interesting Ideas
D. Reflections on what I must start doing
E. Reflections on what I must stop doing
F. Reflections on what I must continue to do

Each month, each executive needs to summarise their entries into a small Report, and sit with their immediate Line Manager – and this is minuted and logged in the employee database – and summarised for their annual development appraisal. Only those who have done this fully are given the opportunity to gain access to the external training Programs the organisation provides. If this process is adopted, you 'force' reflections – and peg it as a pre-requisite for development, in which the organisation invests money. This enforces the principle that YOU need to WANT TO grow before you are invested in, for development – a win-win for both the organisation and the individual. This will also enable you to discern between those who WILL put in the time and effort and those who do not and also, involve Line Managers in having ongoing development conversations and dialogues with their Team members.

Learning how to influence and impact others is essential for any Leader. In fact, the entire premise of Leadership is that titles and 'formal authority' are *not* what Leadership is about. Rather, it is about influence and positive impacts. How do we learn to influence others positively? How can we learn this through self-reflection, observations, deductions and thought-through action?

An interesting idea to play with was something we observed at one of the Development Centres conducted for one of our clients. The Development Centre was done in order to ascertain the Competencies of a select group within a large HR team in order to develop a series of development initiatives for them to be grown into more Senior Roles within the organisation. The feedback for each Participant was based on several external observers who each made commentaries about each candidate they observed, across 8 activities and role plays. What was interesting was what the HR Director did after collating all the observations and feedback. He got each candidate to come in, and fill in a detailed questionnaire which had the following areas (commenting on each individual Participant who took part in the DC):

A. *What are your general observations about the individual?*
B. *How did YOU influence them in the activities – what do you think the best-influencing strategy was? (It had to be listed PER Participant they interacted with.)*
C. *How did THEY influence YOU? (Once again, each Participant's strategies were to be listed and rated.)*
D. *What did YOU learn about influencing and impacting others?*
E. *Which 'tactics' will you apply in your daily work going forward?*

We thought this was a brilliant little activity on self-reflection, and used this as part of some of our Leadership Development Programs, with great success. We curate little activities where we encourage Participants to work with each other quite closely and observe how they influence each other – and what they prefer most and what they prefer least – and facilitate a common forum to discuss learning. This enables Participants to understand that influencing is quite different to 'ordering' or 'commanding' others – and also – internalise key influencing strategies they learn by observing themselves and others.

Being able to understand consciously that different personalities will require different 'pressure points' to be used to successfully influence them – and also – to understand that you, in turn, are most likely to be influenced by your own preferences, is an important learning in the Leadership journey. Self-Reflection and the conscious questioning of these aspects enable Leaders to make notes, reflect and internalise.

Ultimately, all of Leadership can be summed up into:

- Observation,
- Deduction,
- Action, and
- Reflection.

You should be able to observe what is – as is – and the inter-relationships, you must be able to deduce the impacts and possible impacts and play in your mind the interconnected action that is required; then, you must be able to take action based on the deductions made, with the full appreciation that whatever action you take will have repercussions – and that you need to be able to 'deal with it' and then of course, you need to be able to reflect on it, learn from it, and course-correct as required as the contexts and situations change. Sounds simple – and it is – but simple does *not* mean *easy*.

There really is no need to complicate Leadership. It is an intersection between thought and action, you and others, actions and results.

Being able to understand Leadership in simple terms matters, so you do not get overwhelmed by it. It is also important to be able to *focus* on *what matters* rather than getting caught up in all the 'fads and the fluff.' Simplifying Leadership is not about dismissing theories, frameworks, or concepts – it is about seeing the *fundamentals* in all of it – and being able to bring it to a place of action, rather than making it the domain of philosophic debate. Leadership in organisations is about the *doing* of it – more than the debate of *what it should be*.

Once again – this is not something that can be *taught* – but needs to be *learnt* instead. Coupled with seeing Leadership as 'observation, deduction, action and reflection' it is important to understand the *core* things you *must* learn as a Leader (at a personal level) which, through our observations, discussions, assignments and work for the past twenty years amount to four things:

- Discipline
- Focus
- Resilience
- Learning to follow *and* Lead

Most people chase the 'follow your passion' rabbit hole without focusing on Discipline first. Being disciplined – in thought, word and deed is the most fundamental building block for a Leader. Without you being able to discipline yourself, there really is no hope of leading anyone or anything else.

The second is the intensity of focus. Focus – and being able to remain focused – amidst all the 'noise', is what enables Leaders to be 'on track' rather than veer off course and go around in circles without really making any headway.

Resilience is essential because almost nothing goes exactly according to plan. It is essential to be able to 'roll with it' and have it in you to keep getting back up in the face of adversity, challenges, and failures. Without resilience, many Leaders simply give up – and worse still – become warped.

Finally, Leaders need to learn to lead *and* to follow. This is critical. Most of the time, Leaders are not 'taught' to follow – nor do they learn it instinctively as many see following as the antithesis of Leadership, rather than an integral part of it. Being able to understand leading and following as interchangeable and complementary roles and both *not* being based on a title or a hierarchy is important, to appreciate *what* to learn as a student of Leadership. This *one* simple differentiation – seeing leading *and* following as skills to learn and develop, makes you a more wholesome and often far more effective Leader.

So, enabling learning of Discipline, Focus, Resilience and Learning to Lead and Follow needs to be a definitive focus in whatever intervention is planned – and also – there needs to be a form of impetus for the individual to do so as well. At the same time, self-learning - from the individual's perspective – must be 'aligned' to these elements – lest what you learn does not really add value.

Self-Learning needs to add value – and it is important to ensure that whatever is learnt is also directed towards the development of a 'whole' Leader – not just someone who either performs superlatively *or* is a fantastic human being. Being *both* is critical. Often times there is a lob sided effort – those who focus on values let go of bad performance – those who focus on performance turn a blind eye to values. Leadership is not an either/or – it is an *and*.

One of the most delightful examples where we had the privilege of observing this at play is at Dankotuwa Porcelain. Dankotuwa Porcelain is a household Sri Lankan brand with a rather good reputation overseas as well. The company has seen a few changes in ownership and dismal financial performance for more than half a decade. The new CEO Channa Gunawardena introduced a rather radical initiative that was a shining example of creating a framework and a structure for collective Leadership – and through it – encouraging self-development as Leaders. Channa broke the entire Senior and Middle Management Teams into 6 groups, and gave each group the 'charge' of 'running the business' for two months each. Each group is given complete autonomy to make decisions (as long as they are within budgets agreed to together at the beginning of the year). Each group also 'feedbacks' to the group they are handing over – and key 'lessons learnt' are discussed weekly and in-depth monthly. The entire Team was collectively held responsible for overall performance – and their increments and bonuses pegged to both the two months they were directly responsible for – and 30% to the average performance overall business meeting objectives set.

The business achieved its BEST RESULTS in the HISTORY of the company in 2021 and in 2022 Channa gave the opportunity for the next tier groups - including selected 'Supervisors' (who are non-executive category employees) the opportunity to lead the overall organisation as well – and made the ENTIRE senior Teams' overall bonus be pegged 20% to THAT Team succeeding in their two months of Leadership – forcing the helping of their Juniors to succeed.

This daring 'experiment' in collective and distributed Leadership had a wonderful feedback loop built in – coupled with a self-reflection framework executed informally - that made this a perfect example of how to LEARN leading and following along with observation, deduction, execution, and reflection. Channa personally sits with almost all individuals in the groups, both formally at the meetings, and also, importantly, informally over a social drink, a coffee or sometimes a ride back home. During these meet-ups, there are constant and 'featured' questions – which are:

A. *So... How do you read the next few months?*
B. *Do we have everything in place to perform?*
C. *If YOU could change anything immediately – what would it be?*
D. *WHY have you NOT changed it so far?*
E. *What HELP do you need from ME to make it happen?*
F. *What does it tell YOU about YOURSELF – given that you have NOT done ANYTHING about it so far?*
G. *So... shall we agree on X, Y, and Z as being done by A, B, and C?*
H. *Tell me – what should I do if you DON'T do these?*
I. *Do you think YOU are the best person to lead this? If not, who would you propose?*
J. *What help do you need to lead? What do you think you need to do to learn how to follow better?*

Channa's conversations are a great example of coupling performance coaching and Leadership coaching. These are almost never structured or 'minuted' or 'planned' – he does it as and when he has time – but he does it regularly. Everyone knows that a 'conversation' will happen – and many know *exactly* what is going to be asked – as it is almost always the same. They also know that BS will simply be drilled down until both parties know that it is BS going around. So, no one falters in calling things out as they see it. Channa doesn't take any offence in anything being said – but – dovetails back to, So... What do *you* think *we* should *do* – and holds them accountable to whatever that is said. Channa's insanely good memory makes writing things down unnecessary – and whenever the follow-up conversation happens, he starts with what was 'agreed' – which often catches many by surprise the first time. However, now, *everyone* brings a notebook with them when they sit with Channa – and happily makes notes of what they agree with – lest they are caught by surprise by Channa (which he mischievously does ever so often – just to impress upon his Team the importance of *knowing* what *exactly* was *agreed* to.)

This process, continuously done over 18 months, has made a Team that has begun to observe deeply, make deductions after careful deliberation and assessing, take action collectively, and reflect openly and honestly. It has, in a nutshell, created a learning culture that is absolutely perfect for self-learning Leadership – and collectively applying the learning – with peers acting as Mentors and Coaches. In 2022, their performance surpassed their targets and was confirmed to be one of the best years they have had.

The final piece of self-learning is to know the limitations of self-learning and know when to reach out for help. *Always* asking for help stops *you* from thinking things through in your own head. Relying *solely* on *your* thoughts limits your perspectives and insights. *Both* are important. A Coach helps *you* think better; a Mentor helps you learn from them. Both can help – but only *once* you have thought things through for yourself. Learning to be self-reliant is important in Leadership – equally important is knowing when to get help.

Knowing when to do what is an art form that you need to perfect. No one can quite teach you this. However, this is where a good 'boss' really helps. They can guide in both. This is why growing Leaders hinges a lot on having a set of Leaders *across* the organisation that can help grow other Leaders.

Self-learning is something that needs to happen through each individual within the organisation – but once again – it is important to ensure it is propagated and facilitated as well. Left to their own devices, individuals learn – but may well learn the *wrong* principles and habits – which are often very difficult to 'undo.' Especially in the formative years of a young future Leader, it is important to inculcate the habit of self-learning – formally, informally, and also, continuously.

One of the stories I always share during my training Programs is of one of my former bosses who never quite gave 'answers' whenever I had a 'problem.' I found this utterly frustrating initially, taking offence to his Yoda-type riddles and tongue-in-cheek sarcasm levelled against my inability to 'think' – but – soon enough – realised the importance of his 'questioning' in my own development. Here is one such instance.

I was a young Executive and was frustrated over the inability to find the reason for a quality failure that was taking place. Having gone through the reasoning process I was taught, and not having found a solution, I went to him. His question:

'Is this an Executive's problem – or is this a Director's problem? (We didn't have a Manager at the time – so, he was the one we went to for all 'problems.')

I came back – knowing that this was my 'problem' to solve. Having spent another day without a solution – I went back to him – only to be asked the same question.

After two days of being sent back without a solution, I lost my cool and told him, 'I think you don't know the answer yourself – which is why you are sending me from pillar to post!'

He invited me to have a smoke with him (I didn't realise he smoked till then – later I realised he didn't smoke as a habit – but knowing that I did, decided to have that 'occasional fag' knowing I would possibly be at my 'calmest' having a smoke!)

Having a smoke bummed from me, he calmly told me, 'You know Vidusha, I understand your frustration.

However, do know that I don't appreciate that tone of voice. And yes, by the way, it is still YOUR problem.'

He made me work on a solution for an entire week until I arrived at it. Unbeknown to me, he had made sure that the customer was informed, extensions sorted, and the 'ramifications' of the delay were sorted out. ONCE I had found the solution, he sat me down, and took me through a set of frameworks, including introducing me to the Six Thinking Hats of Dr Edward De Bono and mentored me on how to find solutions using tools – rather than only 'logic' and 'reason' and 'experience.' This made me understand HOW to think – and also – HOW to navigate issues – a lesson I learnt well – and which I practice to this date.

The *same* boss came to my cubicle one day and seeing me with my hands on my head in thought, asked me, 'What are you thinking about?' I explained the problem I was grappling with – and he told me, 'Why not ask X from company Y about it – they have some superb practices around this.'

I looked incredulously at him. I told him, quite amusingly: 'I thought you wanted me to solve my own problems.'

'Yes, Vidusha,' and I still remember the twinkle in his eyes. 'However, this is not a problem within your own domain of expertise. Think about it – that is good – but also – why not *ask* someone who might know better?'

He saw the confusion on my face – and then happily added: 'Seeking your own solutions is important. Asking for help is also important. *Why choose*? Learn to do *both*!'

I must admit I honestly thought he was merely contradicting himself at the time. However, over time, I have learnt the wisdom of his words.

Chapter 12

Creating Feedback Loops

"There is no positive or negative feedback – there is only feedback – how you take it makes it positive or negative."

Throughout the last few chapters, there is a common and recurring thematic – which binds all forms of learning and development – which is of *feedback.* Feedback is fundamental to the growth of Leaders across the hierarchy.

However, for feedback to work, both the person giving feedback and the one who receives it need to have some fundamentals committed to it. Feedback – like many things – will be quite inefficient and counterproductive without frameworks and structures in place first.

In developing Leaders, the biggest focus is generally on those *giving* feedback. And though there certainly is merit to this, I have often felt this should not be the case. The reason is simple: feedback matters more to the person getting it. Unless those who are 'benefitting' from feedback are oriented and trained in how to 'receive' feedback *first* and *foremost* then, I believe, what we create is a rather 'shallow' and 'sterile' set of feedback statements unilaterally imposed, which is not what is best to grow Leaders.

Here are some fundamental paradigms we need to shift[1]:

From the giver's perspective:

- Feedback needs to be Positive
- Feedback must be always given using Coaching frameworks
- Feedback needs to be Formal
- Feedback needs to be Fact-based
- Feedback must be from Superiors
- Feedback needs to be Fair

It is important to understand that though *ideally*, feedback needs to be positive, based on coaching frameworks, fact-based and fair, as well as done formally to ensure actions afterwards can be discussed, this 'idealism' becomes counterproductive to helping access the massive gains which derive from treating feedback as feedback.

1 Feedback from superiors is instrumental in assessing performance and guiding career advancement. As previously discussed, peer feedback offers valuable insights into one's organisational standing and potential blind spots.

Not everyone's feedback *needs* to be structured, cautious or positive. In fact, there is genuine merit in teaching everyone to be *open* to feedback of *any* sort. Sometimes, pointed, harsh and critical feedback IS required. Sometimes that is *exactly* what is needed to grow. Sometimes, sadly, it is what we also *never give* in sterile and 'politically correct' environments. Often, we look at such feedback as 'toxic' – and actively discourage the giving of it.

Think of sports – the inspirational origin of Coaching. Think of the best Coaches. Do you see them calm, composed, always positive and having 'meaningful' dialogues – or do you see them waving their hands about – often being abusive and hysterically harsh, downright nasty at times? Why is it that you think athletes THRIVE under these Coaches – often building hugely respectful and lifelong friendships with them? Watching 'The Final Shot' – the story of Tony Parker, I mused what Tony's Coach would have been like in Corporate Settings – would he still be effective – or would he possibly be dismissed for such aggressive behaviour?

This is not for a moment advocating the other extreme of abusive and toxic 'bosses' who think 'anything goes.' The *key* is this: every player who comes to play for a Coach trusts the Coach instinctively, and understands that the Coach and they have a common purpose – to win the championship. Towards this – whatever the Coach gives as 'feedback' is taken positively – and worked on – because that baseline trust and confidence is established.

Some of the *best* feedback is often harsh – often curt – often hard – and often offered in the heat of the moment. This is the norm in almost all sports. The 'Coach' is almost always the one to give it – and the 'players' don't really have a 'choice' in it. Once again, this is *not* to say this needs to be replicated completely in corporate settings – *but* – there *is* a lesson to learn from its effectiveness.

We need to *teach* everyone to be able to *take* feedback as feedback – and forget the 'way' feedback is given. There is a wonderful phrase in Buddhism that goes something like this (loosely translated – much more eloquent and poetic in Sinhalese[2].)

"No matter HOW the speaker speaks
The 'listener' must LISTEN with wisdom."

This is possibly the best advice to be given to anyone who is serious about considering feedback a gift, and being able to benefit from it. Many things are said by way of feedback which we dismiss either because of *who* is saying it, and more often because of *how* it is being said. So, if feedback loops are to be used effectively in relation to *growing* Leaders, it is important for those receiving feedback to be 'taught' or 'inducted' into *how* to *receive* feedback – and to impress upon them how to *listen* – irrespective of the tonality of voice, the harshness of the sentiment or the unfounded basis of the perception.

2 කියන්නා කෙසේ කීවත්
අසන්නා සිහි බුද්ධියෙන් ඇසිය යුතුය is the Sinhala phrase.

So, here are the simple basics you need to consider, to train anyone on how to 'receive' feedback:

A. Understand that feedback is just that – feedback. Nothing more; nothing less.
B. Understand that feedback is neither positive nor negative – feedback is neutral. Whether it becomes positive or negative is determined by *your reaction* to it. Even the harshest and most vile feedback, if used for your growth and development, becomes a positive thing. The best of feedback, the most heartfelt and carefully worded feedback, not used or simply unactioned, becomes useless and of no worth.
C. Listen to the *content* – what *exactly* is being said. Don't get caught up in the 'manner' in which feedback is given.
D. The *message* needs to take precedence over the *person* or the *style*.
E. You don't have to either agree or disagree with feedback. You don't *have to* act on it, either. If you think the feedback is of no use – you are completely at liberty to simply dismiss it. However, *listening* and *reflecting* on the feedback will offer you – at the very least – an insight into how you are *percieved* within the business/organisation.

Obviously, it is also important to train the 'giver' of feedback on how to do so in a meaningful and constructive manner. There are many models and frameworks for this that one finds in coaching conversations related to training – any one of them is a great place to start. SBI, GROW and other models are all built around the same basic principles, which are:

A. Make the feedback about a specific concern, issue, or situation – never make it 'personal', dismissive or condemnatory.
B. Illustrate *why* you are giving this feedback – and how it impacts a person, situation, or result. Link the 'impact' to the 'situation' so that the individual understands the interconnectedness.
C. Allow the individual to offer their perspectives, insights, and thoughts – never make it a 'monologue.'
D. Ensure there is a 'way forward' discussed and agreed upon.
E. Preferably, follow up – and close the loop once you see progress being made.

Taking on a Coaching-based approach to feedback enables meaningful conversations to take place – and also – to make feedback something people do not cringe at hearing.

Something that is really interesting is that most 'feedback' is given around 'weaknesses' or 'areas of improvement' rather than 'how to augment a strength.' When giving feedback, especially around Leadership-related aspects, or any other behaviour-related aspects, remember that it is easier and faster to grow strengths and augment them than learning to 'overcome weaknesses.' Both are certainly required in your Leadership journey, but don't forget to look at how to augment the core strengths of an individual: giving them the ability to truly harness their innate capabilities – which is obviously something they will enjoy doing – more so than 'improving a weakness.'

It is also important to view feedback as something that needs to be given with context and neutrality in mind. Most of the time, we clearly draw lines between 'good' and 'bad' and between 'strength' and 'weakness'; and it is important to understand that in many, many circumstances, good and bad, right and wrong, strength and weakness are context-related, and not absolutes. It is important that you do not grow Leaders by using 'idealistic' and 'black and white' type approaches: use feedback to have 'conversations' about what 'works for which context' rather than drawing distinctions based on the 'this is the right way to do it' approach.

Relating a summary of a series of conversations that we observed as part of a Leadership development engagement at MAS Holdings highlights the above points. During these conversations, the Line Manager demonstrated the subtle art of making feedback a learning process – and a context-driven process – very well. The background is this: The Coach is a Head of Division who has been with the business for a long time. She is a well-respected individual, and is being identified as someone who would be groomed to take a more senior position in the next 1-2 years. She heads one of the most difficult technical aspects of the business. The Coached is a young up-and-coming executive, earmarked for promotion to an Assistant Manager role in the next promotion cycle. The issue is that, though the individual is a brilliant performer he 'rubs people the wrong way' and often there are complaints about his 'abrasiveness.' Though never quite resorting to filth or bad language or even the raising of voices, the Coached is rather tough in his stances, doesn't give in, and is often called 'impatient.'

The feedback was first collated using a 360-Review process with six key peers with whom he works, five of his immediate subordinates, and also 6 others from different SBUs with whom he interacts, on a regular basis, for Projects and initiatives.

1. *The first session saw the Coached being defensive. He offered a ton of 'excuses' as to why the feedback was 'bad.' He was also clearly extremely annoyed that he was being 'picked on', when all he was trying to do was to ensure that the 'job was done right.' The Coach never insisted on anything – and merely told him to mull over what he thought may have contributed to this feedback. Very importantly, she*

established the fact that feedback was feedback – and that he DID NOT REALLY HAVE TO TAKE IT, if he didn't want to.

2. *The second session saw a more mellowed Coached, who had clearly mulled over the Report, and was discussing things about his own behaviour that may lead to this 'perception' of him. He was still defensive – and many times insisted that he was 'not a bad person' or 'unfair', when he insisted on certain things. Once again, the Coach allowed the 'venting', and contextualised situations, and asked 'Could you have handled these differently?', and got him to think through different approaches for the next session.*
3. *In the next 3-4 sessions, the Coach carefully discussed context-specific responses – and carefully discerned between when to 'put your foot down' and when to 'give in and compromise,' enabling the Coached to understand that BOTH were important.*
4. *Having won him over, and established trust that she was not on a 'witch hunt', she opened up the conversation on what she thought were his strengths – and his reflections on his own strengths – and discussed how he could leverage his strengths to 'help and assist' those who may think he was an 'uncompromising tough nut' (a statement given as feedback which truly upset him, when reading his Report). The Coached clearly understood how he could play to his strengths in being detail-oriented,*

results-oriented and being extremely competent technically to 'solve problems' for others, and that he was capable of being more of a Coach himself: a challenge which he took on, quite eagerly.

5. *The next 3-4 sessions saw the Coached leading the conversations, and discussing openly how he was working on leveraging his strengths, whilst at the same time consciously working on changing perceptions about him, and working on his development.*

Six months later, when the follow-up 360 was done, there was a marked change in perceptions, and many lauded his efforts – and one comment that was truly wonderful to see was 'he is becoming one of those go-to people we rely on for help.'

Feedback continued, but more informally, afterwards. With perceptions changing rapidly and the Coached focusing on using feedback, he was fast-tracked for promotions – and is currently a Manager being identified as a candidate for a Senior Manager position.

Something else that needs to be appreciated is that formal feedback is not the only form of feedback that is needed. Much can also be done by way of informal feedback. In fact, we often have a lot more informal feedback coming our way than the formal variety. As such, only focusing on 'formal feedback' to 'action' things is a mistake. A culture needs to be created where individuals *seek* feedback – and gain insights from all the forms of 'obvious' and 'not so obvious' feedback that they receive.

An interesting experiment in creating feedback loops and encouraging informal feedback 'collection' was seen with one of our clients – a relatively small Team of 200 or so Employees – in the IT/BPO industry. This is still a relatively structured framework – but it gives a great insight into how to link formal and informal feedback – and also how to use it to grow a certain 'self-awareness' among Emerging Leaders.

The Team, usually working in a hybrid work setting, generally does not physically meet – and most of their work is being done online or in small groups. Teamwork is critical for the Teams – and collaboration is critical across Teams. However, given that many have not met each other, perceptions they have of each other are often relatively biased – and often wrong. Many had rather big 'chips on their shoulders' about others – a problem the organisation wanted to 'fix' because it was affecting performance overall.

Rather than taking a formal approach to giving and receiving feedback, they created a small 'get to know your Team members' initiative which saw the use of feedback in a very creative way.

Each week – on a day that is not told in advance, chosen individuals get to give anonymous feedback about identified individuals. Rather than the usual 'what do you like – what don't you like' type questions, the HR Team got creative. They asked various questions, here are some samples:

- *What is my favourite colour?*
- *What sports do I watch regularly?*
- *If I am to get stranded on a lonely island – I hope I get stranded with....*
- *If I were the new boss – I would change these three things*

You catch the drift!

What was really awesome was this: they got the person concerned (about these questions that were asked around) to answer the exact same questions – and got a system to 'match' whose answers were 'closest' to the individual concerned answers. The 'dashboard' came up weekly.

Here is what gets interesting: they got the individuals in the Team to do a small 'reflection' around this feedback, sit with their external Coach (only for those who were identified as potential Leaders within the fold) and go through a series of 'self-reflections' – aimed at understanding how they were perceived, and using the feedback collective informally, though this 'game like' initiative to create 'plans' to 'be seen in a more positive light.' Rather than formal 360 Reviews, this organisation used 'gamification' type feedback loops.

What is important is this. The feedback that we receive – both formally and informally – is used to *grow* the Leaders within the organisation. Feedback comes in all forms – in different ways – through different channels. Being receptive to feedback is important – as is having a way of incorporating it towards having insights into how Leaders are perceived within the business. Across the organisation, if feedback is institutionalised and used as a starting point for reflection and growth – it is actually all you need to truly become an effective, wholesome Leader.

One of our favourite tools, which we observed being used extremely effectively towards feedback being made 'normal', is the 'hot seat' which we often use for many of our signature Leadership Programs.

The hot seat is simple. There is a 'hot seat' in the middle of the room. Around it, in semicircular form (so that you can 'see' each person sitting in front of you) are chairs where others sit. In the 'hot seat' is the recipient of feedback – around him/her are those giving feedback.

Guidelines are given. The receiver of feedback on the 'hot seat' cannot rebut, argue, or defend anything being said. They have to simply listen to the feedback – clarify anything that they did not understand, and thank the others for the feedback after it is done.

Those around, giving feedback, are told to:

- *Be conscious and aware that it is a PERSON who is listening – as such, be sure NOT to say anything hurtful, derogatory, or intensely personal (such as you are too short – you are bald etc.) Feedback needs to be related to their work, relationships, and something that they can DO SOMETHING about.*
- *EACH PERSON sitting around the hot seat needs to give three positives and three negatives about the person on the hot seat (some have only one – others five – the choice is for each organisation/Team to make). No one can give ONLY positives or negatives – everyone needs to give an equal number of positives and negatives.*

The first time we saw this being done, we saw the total discomfort and anxiousness. However, with each passing session, we saw a lot more ease – and also – a lot more seriousness. The 'political correctness' was not there – there was absolute honesty. Some of our clients have institutionalised this after each management meeting, and they tell us that it has really enabled a greater appreciation for each individual – and also paved the way to see a lot of self-reflection and improvement because of it. The ability to give feedback 'face to face', and see that their Manager ALSO takes feedback –

makes this process doubly effective. However, everyone who has done this tells us one simple thing – IF there is a REACTION to the feedback AFTERWARDS – especially by a Manager – trust is completely shattered, and no one really gives proper feedback. So, having the right mindset and culture is critical before implementing these initiatives. Feedback – especially pointed and critical feedback – is ONLY effective in learning environments; in other contexts, it actually causes more harm than good.

Chapter 13

The Role of Encouragement, Punishment & Removal in Growing Leaders

"Without hell, heaven is meaningless. Without heaven, hell is meaningless."

We often debate the merits of 'positive and negative' reinforcement and whether the 'carrot' or the 'stick' works better. Though there is a growing tendency to lean more towards 'encouragement' and 'engagement' and 'motivation' and 'enabling' Leaders, it is important to understand that growing Leaders within the organisation requires *both* avenues to be explored – and also set in place. Thinking that people respond *only* to positives and that Leaders can be grown without *any* punishments or negative impacts is being naive.

The reason is simple. *If* you are rewarding the right behaviour, there must be punishment for the 'wrong' behaviour. *Not* experiencing any repercussion for breaking of values, unacceptable behaviour, and misdemeanours is a sure way of sending out a message loud and clear that 'it does not matter' – which is the wrong message to send. Without a consequence, there is a culture of 'anything goes' which is *not* conducive to growing Leaders – at least Leaders who are effective, wholesome and true role models for others.

What you do, and what you don't do, are both important in Leadership – a lesson that needs to be instilled in Leaders across the organisation. No one is above the Code – no one is exempt from repercussions, and everyone needs to 'play by the rules.' Unless this is established – without a doubt – without question – the culture you create is a rather misaligned and hypocritical one – which more often than not, leads to toxicity. As such, ensuring there are 'punishments' is as important as having schemes and frameworks for praise, recognition, and encouragement.

The purpose and intent of the 'punishment' and the 'way' in which it is meted out are important to consider. Often, the 'letter of the law' is followed without the 'spirit of the law' being present. Remember – the role of 'punishment' is to be both a deterrent and also, a way of ensuring equity and Fair Play across the organisation. Punishments should not be a 'way of life' and a 'first resort' – they must always be weighed in on, enacted with decorum and respect, and above all, even *in* punishment – the focus must be to *grow Leaders* – *not* to discard people or give up on them as 'failures'.

Can you PUNISH someone and STILL ENABLE LEARNING? Certainly, sounds paradoxical – but, as with most aspects of growing Leaders, it doesn't necessarily have to be. One of the most poignant lessons in following the rules, punishing, and STILL helping grow Leadership is something I personally observed through Mr Aslam Omar – the Managing Director of Phoenix Industries – and the brother of Ashroff Omar – the Managing Director of Brandix – One of Sri Lanka's leading apparel manufacturers.

Mr Aslam (as he is known by all) is one of those people who has a rather unique way of 'teaching' – and many – including myself – have been fortunate enough to be 'unofficially' mentored and tutored and groomed by him. During an assignment for Phoenix, Mr Aslam gave me the charge of two Management Trainees. Both were qualified, competent and extremely talented. I favoured one – simply because he seemed to have a bit more 'spunk' than the other – but they were both equally poised – and I knew only one of them could move forward – and be groomed to be the next Head of HR for the company. Then, quite unexpectedly, one of them was found guilty of breaking a somewhat sacred rule – and it was clear that 'something had to be done.' Not wanting to ruin a young career – but at the same time – charged with having to 'lay down the rule book', Mr Aslam knew there was a dilemma that he could possibly weigh in on. I remember him taking me to his cubicle at Head Office, and our having a smoke together, and him asking me: 'What do you think I should do?' – he purposefully emphasised the 'I', making sure he made me understand that whichever way this goes, he was lending weight to it.

I told him I saw no way out. Given that the 'crime was committed' I told Mr Aslam that the 'time needs to be done' but added 'I must admit, I hate having to do it.' Mr Aslam sat there for some time finishing his cigarette, and then laughed – and told me with a twinkle in his eye, 'YOU are the HR Man – YOU should be able to look at all of this to help people grow.' And then, as was quite characteristic of him – he put a twist to things – that generally makes all of us sit and think about it for time to come.... He told me that just because you take ACTION AGAINST someone, it does not have to be done in a 'doomsday' manner. Sure, the deed was done – and there was no going back – but one mistake – whether intentional or not – does NOT have to mean a 'permanent black mark.' I wasn't quite sure where he was going with all the philosophic undertones – but I understood it when he took action – which I was fortunate to be privy to – as it completely changed my mindset about 'taking action.'

Mr Aslam sat with the young man, and explained the situation – but never asked him whether he did it or not. Given that the inquiry was held, judgment passed and decisions made – he never bothered with the formalities.

However, he explained to the young man that this needs to be a lesson learnt – for life – for all time – and never to be repeated. He stressed on how much potential he saw in him – and how much he still believed in him. He also told him that 'mistakes are fantastic opportunities to learn – and grow.' Upon the young man tendering his resignation, Mr Aslam spoke to the young man again, and gave him an opportunity at another company he oversaw – with full disclosure about the disciplinary action taken at Phoenix – and personally taking accountability were it to be repeated. Many, including me, spoke to Mr Aslam about the 'precedent' it sets. But, he smiled like he usually does, laughed and told me 'That's a good precedent isn't it? It shows that we don't stop believing in people's potential!' Today, the young man is a celebrated HR Director – who not only learnt invaluable lessons through his mistakes – but also – used it to grow and move forward. Mr Aslam could have ended that career, but he didn't. He used it to help grow Leadership in the young man, and in doing so, taught US who were around him how to use EVERYTHING as an opportunity to grow Leadership – rather than destroy it.

Not all mistakes are the same. Sometimes, horrendous oversights happen: sometimes some individuals intentionally do wrong by the organisation; sometimes, there is pure cussedness and blatant disregard for decency. Sexual Harassment, Embezzlement, Fraud: these are not just misdemeanours or 'mistakes' or 'opportunities to teach Leadership' – or are they?

Whenever 'situations' happen – no matter how extreme it is – two things *must* happen:

- Due process *must* take place. Taking action *without* due process is as bad as overlooking it.
- Whatever action is taken, you need to be civil, decent and professional about it.

Everyone has a right to their dignity – even someone who has committed a crime. Ensuring this humanity prevails is important in Leadership – and can only be learnt if there are reference points to it from our own experience. Mr Aslam's approach to handling the issue with the young Management Trainee is something that we *all* learnt from. Had we never been privy to such incidents, we too would possibly take a much more 'cold' approach to meting out punishments – devoid of humanity – devoid of dignity – and thereby, devoid of learning – with only ill feelings and extreme prejudice resulting. Being able to 'rise above' is critical to good Leadership. Being able to be a human being first is critical to good Leadership. Being able to learn – and teach – even in the most difficult of circumstances is important to good Leadership. In fact, it is in these times we learn the most endearing and inightful of all lessons in Leadership.

So, never shy away from taking the tough calls – but remember to work with the end in mind – the end being to grow a Leader, *not* to simply mete out a punishment and follow due process.

Possibly THE MOST extreme example I can cite from personal experience is that of Reverend Samuel J. Ponniah's brother being stabbed and killed at our Alma Mater. I was in the UK following my undergraduate studies when a letter arrived with the news of this harrowing incident. Father Sam's brother (who was a student at the time – and the reverend was NOT a reverend back then – simply a young old boy who was teaching in College) intervened to stop a scuffle between two parties after an event in College – and was stabbed in the process. He died in Father Sam's arms en route to the hospital.

Though many ganged up to seek retribution and 'justice' Father Sam's father – who was also a reverend was very very clear in his sermon at his son's funeral. Violence begets violence. Hatred begets hatred. An eye for an eye makes the whole world blind. It is only through love and forgiveness that it all ends. Being a 'Christian', he urged everyone to respect his son, and his legacy, and NOT take matters into their own hands. Though many of us struggled to accept this was 'God's Will' I remember sitting down and reflecting, and writing home to my dad about the whole incident – and my father writing back to me saying, 'He is a better Buddhist than many Buddhists I know.'

This one incident is still etched in my mind – because – for once – someone who had directly been affected in the most horrific way was able to forgive, and live by a higher ideal, and demonstrate the true meaning of humanity. THIS was leading by example: given that he was a priest and 'preached' about love and forgiveness and respect. To this day, both Father Sam and his Father possibly have more respect and credibility than anyone else we know; simply because they were able to live by a higher ideal and humanity than what is possible for most of us in a similar circumstance.

What I learnt was this: EVEN in EXTREME circumstances, the purpose of any action should be to 'move forward' as a 'human being' rather than resort to the same vile atrocities as the person committing the crime itself. Two wrongs never make a right is something that was only a sentence to me, till then.

Many years afterwards, when Mr Aslam took certain actions (the young MT was only one of many incidents of this nature) it dawned on me that there was a striking similarity in the 'approach' that Mr Aslam took. Irrespective of the 'crime', Mr Aslam was able to look 'beyond' it, and look at it from the perspective of a 'person' who was entitled to their 'dignity' and 'respect.' Unlike the Reverend, in corporate settings 'forgiveness' is not possible – depending on the 'crime' – so, due process and punishment were always implemented; but what Mr Aslam's approach did was to ensure that 'humanity' was never lost during these episodes – nor the opportunity to teach – with the hope that they learn from it, grow from it, and hopefully, become better because of it. The intention – even when sacking a person – was to help them grow and become better. This, in many ways, is the epitome of the 'inculcating' Leadership – not only in those who commit a crime, but also in those who 'mete out' the 'punishments.'

Sadly, praise, recognition and encouragement are also in short supply to grow Leaders. Many times, with much focus on engagement and employee wellbeing, the type of recognition and praise is becoming something that is 'diluted' in that, it is given without *real* focus on it being deserved. As much as praise, recognition and encouragement are needed – it is a mistake to do so in an 'offhanded' and thoughtless fashion. Unless recognition is placed right, unless praise is for the worthy, and encouragement is backed with a clear focus on improvement, Leaders learn the 'wrong' lessons.

Here are some considerations:

A. Praise needs to be for those who deserve it: for work well done, for key accomplishments, for effort purposefully made, for individuals who truly go above and beyond; not for 'doing something' or doing the 'bare minimum.' This leads to mediocrity, and a culture of accepting the 'average' as 'acceptable.'
B. Recognition needs to be fair, equitable, and merit-based. Without clear, data-driven performance indicators or assessment methodologies, recogni-

tion often becomes mere 'favouritism', and nothing much more.

C. Encouragement must be based on effort being put in, first. Simply 'giving chances' and 'hoping to see improvement' is not going to cut it.

D. Any form of positive reinforcement must be attached to deep observations, proper assessments and a genuine focus on improvement. It is *not* a feel-good factor.

See, you grow Leaders through hard work, honest effort, diligent focus and conscientious involvement. Leadership is not an easy ride – nor is it about 'making it easy' – Leaders are *not* made without trial, blood, sweat and toil. It is not for the faint hearted – nor for those who are not willing to put in the effort. Leadership is not something you 'have' it is something you have to 'grow' over time.

The *support* given to Leaders is not to 'cover for them' nor to 'shield them' or to 'protect' them; it is to *grow* them. As much as a plant will *not* grow in the shade – as much as the grass is *always* greener when you have a ton of hot sun and a great rainfall, Leaders *grow* only through trials and tribulations, and when they are *supported* to learn through them all. This is quite different to simply 'performing well' which is the fundamental mistake many make. Too many times, the *sole* focus is about 'not making a mistake' rather than 'making mistakes and learning from them.' Too many times, the focus is on 'hitting the numbers *somehow*' – rather than 'learning to hit the numbers *with* the support and growth of others' – not simply pushing and shoving and riding roughshod over values and decency. Many who never understand the difference get promoted for their superior performance, and then are found sorely lacking in Leadership, and thereby become extremely weak Managers who eventually grind the organisation to a halt because of the toxic environments they create. So, praise, recognition and support should be directed at *growing Leaders*, not simply ensuring performance. A small distinction here; Please note that at *no point* is performance *not* to be focused on. Ensuring performance is *fundamental* to the organisation – and is not up for debate. The only debate here is on *how* performance is achieved.

Why praise? Why recognition? Simple! It achieves two very basic – yet very important objectives:

A. It makes the recipient feel good – and encourages them to continue to do whatever they are doing – it encourages 'repeat performance.'
B. It also has an effect on the onlookers – and they too want to be recognised and praised. This drives the 'right' behaviour across the organisation.

Praise and Recognition need to be looked at, in both formal and informal methodologies. *Both* are needed.

Sample framework for Formal and Informal Ways of Praise and Recognition

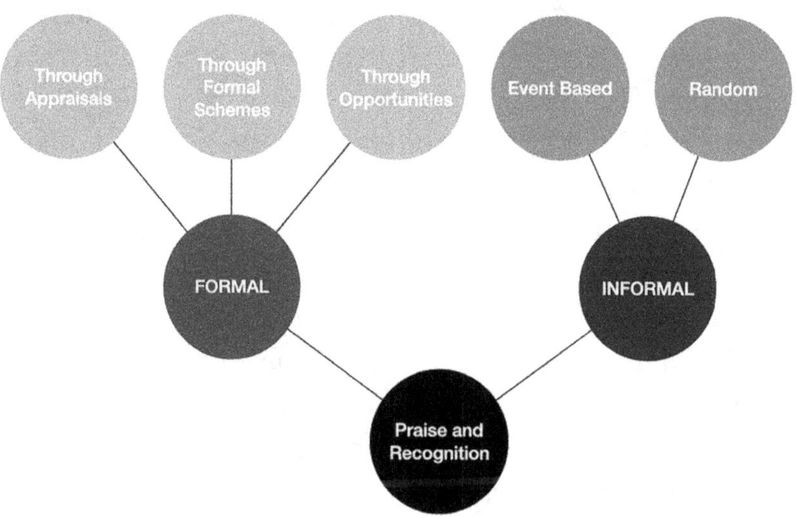

Both are effective. Don't try and choose between the two - invest in *both*.

Have formal frameworks to make sure focused Leadership growth takes place.

Appraisals are a great tool to have to assess rewards and recognise Leadership. Don't confuse this with performance appraisals – this is *not that*. Performance Appraisals are performance appraisals – leave it be. Have Leadership Appraisals, too. The aim and objective of a 'Leadership Appraisal' are to assess Leadership skills and competencies – *not* performance per se. These appraisals give a clear 'message' to the organisation that developing your Leadership skills is important and that it *will* be assessed as much as your performance for you to be considered for future growth within the business.

A well-rounded framework for assessing the 'suitability' of potential candidates for growth into Leadership positions has been developed within the John Keells Group (the largest blue-chip organisation in Sri Lanka). The Assessment Centre John Keells carry out is both intensive and robust and it is DIRECTLY based on the Leadership Competency Framework developed for the entire group. Irrespective of which division or section of the business you belong to – or sector – you are assessed on your Leadership potential and behaviour. Here are some interesting assessment methodologies they adopt (some have been kept back for confidentiality and Non-Disclosure related reasons.)

A. A 360 is done.

B. There is a Case Study – and an interview based on the Case Study.

C. There are group activities.

D. There is also a simulated entrepreneurship challenge – one year the Participants were told to sell 'ice cream' and another group 'frozen meats' at their supermarket premises. The Teams had to ideate a strategy – and then execute it.

The assessment centre is presided over by skip-level Managers who are inducted, oriented, and trained on the assessment centre methodologies and also, given structured formats to follow to write their observations, comments and marks on. They are NOT averaged out – EACH observers/assessors marks, comments and notes are tabulated. The assessment centre involves both internal AND external assessors and observers.

What is awesome is that the results of the 360 are triangulated with the observations Case Study, Group Activities and the Simulated Project. At the 'debrief' they are actually shown all results, observations and comments, and the Participants are involved in the process of asking 'What do these results mean to you?' and also 'How do you develop as a Leader?' The final outcome of the Assessment Centre is a Personal Development Plan for EVERYONE – irrespective of whether they are moved forward within the ranks or not. UNLESS they demonstrate Leadership capabilities, they are NOT given more senior roles within the business units.

These Appraisals offer a huge form of recognition and praise to those who 'pass' and thereby 'move up.' Within John Keells it is absolutely clear that you do NOT move forward UNLESS you hone your Leadership skills. You are not INVITED for the Assessment Centre UNLESS your performance was above average – but you do NOT get promoted unless your Leadership skills were assessed to be 'adequate' for the more senior role you are to move into.

Another important facet within the JKH Assessment Centre framework is this: UNLESS the PDP is completed, they cannot come into another Assessment Centre. So, there is a definitive focus not only on being 'assessed' but on 'growing skills' as well.

Having specific recognition schemes can also play a big role in offering focus and attention to Leadership development. Reward schemes for performance and aspects like innovation are quite common – it is a good idea to take the same approach to recognising and rewarding 'Leadership' as well. This does *not* have to be a separate 'scheme' per se – but can easily be incorporated into the 'awards night' type events currently in place within the organisation.

Here are some interesting examples from some of our Clients who weaved recognising 'Leadership' within their 'gala nights' generally held once a year.

A. The 'Most Admired Leader' award. One of our clients held a 'nomination' process with some interesting questions posed to bring in 'applications' for the award – and got the entire organisation to vote for the selected candidates.

B. The 'Living Values' award. This award was given to anyone who demonstrated exemplary behaviour with regard to values. They told Employees to write in 'stories' which were 'attested for' about anyone they felt had truly lived the organisational values.

C. 'Mentor/Coach/Trainer' awards. Each year MAS recognises internal Employees who volunteered their time to train and develop others. They are given awards – and also – on a few occasions – some 'time off' as a 'thank you'

D. Most Respected Peer award. This was possibly the most coveted award in this client's awards night. Each 'tier' of the organisation voted for the person they respected the most amongst their peers.

These types of awards reward and recognise different aspects of Leadership – and get the entire organisation involved in placing that recognition on them. It creates that much-needed impetus to ensure that 'Leadership' is at the fore – not just performance.

Praise and Recognition can come by way of offering better opportunities and exposure to those who are 'worthy' as well. In many organisations, the type of opportunities are tied to the 9 box grid – and the placement thereof. Ensuring that those who demonstrate Leadership potential are given opportunities to grow their skills and have more exposure is also a great 'communication' to the rest of the organisation that Leadership matters – and that you need to demonstrate the right behaviour in order to be grown further within the organisation.

Once again, the principle is that you need to put in effort for your own development – and this is recognised with further development opportunities. This enables the propagation of making that conscious effort to grow as a Leader – as much as perform in the workplace.

The many examples cited in previous chapters offer an opportunity to understand that organisations that create the environments for Leaders to grow do so by ensuring development is pegged to the effort being made by Employees to learn and practice Leadership. Hirdaramani making self-learning a contingent on coming for the workshops, John Keells' insistence of ensuring the PDP is completed *before* coming in for the next Assessment Centre, Dankotuwa Porcelain's pegging of the Junior levels performance to Senior Levels' bonus and further development initiatives are all based on this principle – that recognition of Leadership behaviour is what enables them to have access to exposure, further development and further training. The message they send out to the rest of the employee population is clear: focus on Leadership development – not just performance.

As much as having formal frameworks for encouragement, praise, recognition and encouragement is essential. It is important to appreciate that the informal and unstructured opportunities should not be overlooked or underplayed. In fact, every single day there are countless opportunities to grow Leaders through praise, recognition and encouragement.

These can be event-based or purely random. Event-based opportunities are when an individual has demonstrated good behaviour or strong Leadership. It is important that such praise and recognition be immediate, instant, and necessarily 'public.' Not all praise needs to be public but it certainly helps when it is. When an individual is praised for something they did – and it is immediate – it has a tremendous impact both on the individual and those around them.

Brandix had a 'card' system. They had cards which were blank - which had the company logo and insignia beautifully printed on the back. Any time something praiseworthy was seen/observed by an employee, one of these cards with a handwritten note was given either immediately, or on the following day's 'morning meeting'

In this digital age, Andrew Strotter Brooks – the Senior Vice President of Learning and Development for Etihad Airways, uses LinkedIn to do the same. Almost on a daily basis, he will post about someone who went 'over and beyond' and post about it – making it something that is not just recognised within the organisation – but seen by the whole world. These 'little' posts draw huge attention, and lots of comments and kudos – propagating the living of values, and the development of the Leadership ethos.

What is important, irrespective of the medium used, is to draw attention to the deed and the impact it created. This 'storytelling' helps create a series of 'lores' around Leadership and Leaders enabling the creation of a Leadership culture within the organisation.

Remember once again: what is celebrated is propagated.

Apart from event-based recognition, there can be absolutely random recognition as well. These can include activities done outside the organisation which demonstrated Leadership, and also, brought a certain impact to either society at large or to a community.

Whether it is event-based or random, being able to *spot* what is *worthy* of recognition is important. Remember – if you only recognise something that is *not* worthy, you truly dilute the effect praise and recognition can have in spurring others on. It also raises eyebrows about your intentions in recognising these in the first place. So, ensure you praise and recognise what is truly worthy – and teach senior and mid-tier Leaders how to discern between what is and what is not worthy.

Chapter 14

Types of sponsors leaders need for them to grow

"No one makes it alone.
At some point, we all need someone's help."

Leaders, especially when they are *becoming* Leaders, need Sponsors to help them grow. A fun fact: though we generally think that trees 'compete' with each other to grow, research finds that there is a complex and interconnected 'collaboration' between trees and other plants in forests. For example, 'Mother Trees' are seen to 'share' their excess nutrients with 'younger trees' – and 'nurture' them to reach their potential[1].

'Sponsoring' talent is critical for young Leaders to grow and be assured that they are 'safe' during their formative years. Without this 'protection' and 'nurture' many who

1 https://vimeo.com/319999556

would possibly become excellent Leaders in their own right simply fall into oblivion, and often never quite blossom as Leaders; choosing rather to simply advance in their career ladder as relatively minor players, without growing as Leaders.

There is a delicate balance needed here. On the one hand, it is important to ensure that 'safety' is provided. On the other hand, it is also equally important to 'push the limits' and get young Leaders out of their 'comfort zones', as this is the only way Leaders can be grown. Even though this is seen as paradoxical, it is not: in fact, it is absolutely complementary; and necessary.

Sponsors are required at all levels though many types of Sponsors remain common across the hierarchical levels. What is important is that Leaders have the sponsorship required to grow and become better Leaders. Sponsorship may not always be within the organisation; you may need outside help at times too.

There is a big misconception that Leaders are 'self-made' and that the biggest 'characteristic' of a Leader is this very trait: the ability to be self-reliant. This must not be discounted. It is critical that individuals have the ability to become self-reliant and have that 'spark' in them that demands more of themselves. It is important that they *want* to become Leaders, and it is important that they are able to pursue learning and development for themselves. However, this *alone* will never quite work. Without a sponsor, many will never quite reach their potential – and worse still, may lose that 'spark' forever. Once that 'spark' is lost, it is quite tough to 'reignite' it, which is why it is critical that young Leaders are sponsored early on – and supported throughout.

Some critical Sponsors are as follows:

A. **Talent Spotters**: These are Seniors who have a 'knack' for spotting talented individuals and are willing to 'highlight' them to the Senior Management Teams. Talent Spotters are critical because many times 'Juniors' go unnoticed, especially in larger organisations which are geographically dispersed.
B. **Opportunity Creators**: Young Leaders need to have opportunities to grow their skills and competencies, as we have previously discussed. Many Senior Leaders don't look outside their own Teams and units to bring talent in to lead initiatives. The ability to lead cross-functional Projects is a big part of honing Leadership skills, when you are starting. Opportunity Creators are essential Sponsors for young Leaders to have an 'arena' to display their skills.
C. **Confidants**: Having someone Senior to bounce ideas with, tell your troubles to, and discuss insecurities with, without the fear of being judged, is important for the growth of young Leaders especially with regard to their confidence and for them to be 'comfortable in their own skin.' Middle Managers and Senior Managers as well as peers can play the role of a confidante.

D. **Funders**: Sometimes, young Leaders don't have the funding to do certain Projects. They have ideas, but they don't have the funds. Senior Leaders include those who are willing to fund initiatives and Projects and ideas and who are willing to 'put their necks on the line' with the much-needed money. Without funders, many Leaders never get the opportunity to showcase their ingenuity and innovativeness.

E. **The Shields**: There will be many times Leaders fail. The more 'daring' you are, the more the chances for failing and making a real mess of things. This is when 'Shields' come in. Too many times, times of failure become the time when Leaders are simply taken to task and from that point, any hope of them ever putting themselves on the line again is lost. After all, why would you go out of your way only to be simply chastised for doing what you felt was right – and what you felt was needed to be done. Taking a risk needs to be supported. This is why 'Shields' are critical. Shields understand that young Leaders need to be 'protected' to be grown. They will criticise young Leaders privately – but always shield them in the wider organisation. Having this 'protection' enables young Leaders to make bold decisions, and keep trying, rather than simply folding their arms in exasperation and giving up.

F. **The Second Chance Giver**: Sometimes, Leaders mess up really badly. These are make-or-break moments, professionally. Sometimes, we all do

> need that second chance. Sponsorship, especially at a Senior Level, where you are given a second chance, and the opportunity to start again means a lot. This often, grows Leaders who are grateful and more broad-minded than those who have 'breezed through' their careers. Sponsorship at this crucial time, with a sponsor that gives a young Leader a second chance, is important.

Many times, Leaders lack Sponsors who can make all the difference between a Leader being hopeful, open-minded, empathetic, and confident. Remember: we are all products of our own experiences. Why should 'Leaders' be any different? Leaders who were not 'sponsored right' tend to be overly harsh, jaded and oftentimes, unidimensional. Leaders who were sponsored throughout their careers tend to be a lot more open, warm, empathetic and positive about humanity overall.

The type of Leader you grow depends a lot on the Sponsorship you had in crucial moments in your career.

My Mother worked for Bodyline – possibly one of the biggest sewing plants 'under one roof' in the region. Bodyline, when it was being built, was a modern marvel. It was such a sprawling unit – and it was the first bra manufacturing plant on the island, co-invested by Triumph International – the German giant in lingerie.

I was just fifteen or so when she started working at Bodyline, and I would often go to Bodyline and wander around the place. It is here that my love of HR was first discovered and, in many ways, deep-rooted. Watching my Mother and several others be 'sponsored' was something that was etched in my mind forever.

Let me give three examples:

My Mom was a 'Stenographer cum Typist' who moved into being a Secretary after about a decade of working. At Bodyline too she was the Head of HR's Secretary. However, Dian Goonathilake, the Head of HR as well as Sherad Amalean saw in my Mom the ability to 'be more than a Secretary.' They spoke to her several times about it, and when my Mother was adamant that she didn't really want to change 'career paths' they made sure Mom was given opportunities to 'do more' than simply her job. When Mom decided to leave when my Dad retired, she was in charge of all personal files, managed the medical centre for the company, oversaw most company events and also, got involved in organising training at supervisory levels. The exposure made her a much more rounded and skilled person, and also, much of what she learnt by way of organising and administration and collaboration she unknowingly incorporated into her life – and her role as a Mother.

Another person who was 'just a kid' when he first came in was VK – who went on to become one of Sri Lanka's most Senior HR professionals a few decades later, heading some of Sri Lanka's biggest organisations after leaving Bodyline. VK was a 'diamond in the rough' as Mom used to call him. A little unpolished in his English, but superlatively fluent in his Sinhala, VK had a certain flair about him which was identified by Dian very fast. He gave him his first 'leg up' in offering opportunities to showcase his talents, sponsoring him in his initial steps in his career. However, as he grew within the department, VK had several other key Sponsors, including some Senior Managers who shielded him on a few occasions when key mistakes were made. However, the biggest Sponsorship he got was in being given the funding to truly bring some of his key ideas to life, which enabled him to gain a pretty awesome reputation for himself as a truly innovating and 'daring' young Manager who was able to 'get things done.'

Another classic success story is a supervisor (who wished to remain anonymous) who went on to become a Director. When she first joined Bodyline, she hardly spoke English at all. She was also only qualified up to her Advance Level Examinations and came from an extremely humble background. The Production Manager and Quality Manager both became her first Sponsors, giving her the opportunity to learn more than the job role she was assigned, and introduced her to the entire manufacturing process. On several key occasions, she was sponsored to take part in extremely expensive technical training Programs, including exposure overseas. When the technical function was being transitioned, and was going to be headed by a local for the first time, she was given the opportunity to grow into the role, even though she was clearly not fully ready. She was also hand-held and shielded by several key Seniors in the department, who later went on to become her subordinates.

What is amazing about all three individuals is that they all went on to become 'Sponsors' in their own right. All three of them are people who instinctively supported, shielded, funded and grew talent in their own right. They never became 'defensive' or 'threatened' by talent. VK went on to sponsor nearly a dozen individuals whom he personally coached into being senior HR professionals in their own right.

My Mom, in her own little way, supported many Supervisors and Sewing Operatives, most of whom are Managers and Senior Managers who speak to me with great fondness whenever I am at Bodyline for my workshops. The young supervisor who became a Director personally supported over two dozen colleagues who have now taken on Senior Technical roles within Sri Lanka, and also, as expatriates in Bangladesh, India and Vietnam.

Part 4

Harvesting

Harvesting Season is both a joyous and an extremely busy period of time. In fact, even now, in most farming communities, families still come together to support during harvesting[1].

Harvesting is when the entire village comes together to ensure that the paddy is harvested on time, and also threshed and made into 'rice.' It is a time of hard work and toil, and also, a time of celebration. The Sinhala and Tamil New Year coincides with the harvesting time as well, when the 'new rice festival' takes place. It is a time steeped in rituals and rites being performed, and a time to pass down generations of tacit knowledge from one generation to the next.

---

1 Many in my generation, who are in corporates, still ask for leave and go back home to support their fathers' and uncle's during this period. For factories that are situated in paddy cultivation areas, absenteeism generally soars during this period – no matter how much incentive is given!

Traditional Harvesting of rice is back-breaking work. Unlike the preparation of soil, harvesting is something in which many women also take part. Unlike any other time in the entire process, a lot more family involvement happens during this period. Role segregation is non-existent, everyone chips in and harvests the paddy.

Though today the traders are in place to take the harvest into large-scale threshing and milling units, back in the day, the paddy was stored in large clay 'storehouses[2]' and threshing was done by hand and 'sifting' of the 'rice' from the 'chuff' happened by using a '*Kulla*[3]' and the wind which makes the 'chuff' fall further afield from the 'rice.' The threshing happened only when required – and it was common for rice to be threshed daily, making many from villages consider rice that is threshed in mills and 'packeted' being 'not fresh.'

The harvesting period is also a time for reflection and gratitude. Our forefathers were acutely aware that their efforts were only one part of the equation. They were aware that 'Mother Earth' had to support their efforts, and 'bless' them with rain and sunshine in the right proportions at the right time. They were acutely aware that success in agriculture was where human sweat needed to be met with the blessings of the earth. They understood that one without the other never results in a bountiful crop. So, harvesting time sees a flurry of songs

2 Called '*Bissa*'.

3 A large spade-shaped utensil made woven from different types of leaves – most commonly rattan or palmyra.

in verse thanking the 'gods' for their 'blessings' and the 'earth' for its 'bounty.' There is a deep reverence and deep gratitude for 'good fortune' and there is also sincere thanks to everyone who contributed.

As much as we grow Leaders, we need to 'harvest' them too. Leaders need to be able to reach their fullest potential, as much as help others reach their fullest potential. At the same time, when success does come, it is important to be able to have a certain humility about it, rather than leading to the cultivation of arrogance and the 'celebrity' status of Leaders, often at the cost of the collective contribution which every person within the organisation has made towards its success.

Chapter 15

Career Progression and Succession Planning for Leaders

"The best will leave if they see no future."

Careers have two dimensions. First, there is the vertical growth in titles. Second, the much less focused on and often unspoken part of the growth of the person, and their Leadership capabilities. The two are *expected* to happen simultaneously, but often this growth does not happen in this neat way. As much as you don't acquire skills needed to be a good parent simply by being a biological parent, you don't acquire Leadership skills simply because you get promoted to being a Manager or a Senior Manager.

Career growth is certainly needed. However, growth as a *person* is far more important (though under-appreciated in a highly competitive and comparative work environment). Performance is not enough – nor is having the potential enough. Underlying both performance and potential there must be a person of solid character[1]. Unless organisations create pathways to grow people, not just titles, Leaders will never quite grow within their structure.

There are a few interesting parallels to draw and learn from in traditional paddy farming communities around career progression and succession planning. Generally, you start out as an apprentice. You work under the close supervision of a senior farmer and generally work alongside him. You are then given a small plot to work on for yourself. The plot you personally manage over time, and if you demonstrate ability, the plot keeps growing till the point you are not able to do it by yourself. At this point, who works with you on your plot is not based on your tenure or skill as a farmer. In Sri Lanka, farmers are not 'paid' per se. They work on a lot of land and share the produce with co-farmers and the owner (if the owner is not a farmer himself).

Sri Lanka was an agricultural nation, and the traditional farmers were a fiercely proud and independent group of people. Each year, anyone who wants to farm, and is starting out as a farmer gets 'allocated' to a more seasoned farmer based on who the young farmer chooses as their 'senior' and also, whether or not the 'senior' wants you. It cuts both ways. This is a rather weird way of doing

1 Character, while often overlooked, is a fundamental pillar of leadership. For an in-depth exploration of this vital aspect, Craig Wheldon's book, *Leadership: The Art of Inspiring People to Be Their Best*, is highly recommended. (https://craigwhelden.com)

things for someone who looks at it from the outside, but it happens nearly seamlessly almost all of the time. At times, you have 'hands' without a 'plot' and those who are without anyone who 'wants them' are generally taken by the most tenured farmer. There are also situations where there are seasoned farmers who don't have anyone to 'help' them apart from their own family. This means this individual can never quite grow – and often – it is because he is not really 'liked' and is considered 'awful to work with/for' by others. As such, many times, 'arrogant' and self-centred' farmers learn quite quickly to change their ways. Not all farmers are 'nice' – but there is a fine line here. There are many farmers who are hard taskmasters – but they are fair, equitable and great Teachers. So, many are perfectly fine with their 'demand for perfection' and 'hard work' because they know it is in their best interest to learn from the best – and be taught, selflessly.

Unlike in traditional farming, we don't have a choice in selecting the boss we have in organisational settings. This is why it's doubly important to ensure those titled 'Managers' are also Leaders. Unless Managers are able to lead as well – and also, help grow more Leaders, Leadership pipelines dry up quite quickly, and there is a natural attrition of top talent and best Leadership potential.

At the same time, unless there are opportunities for those with Leadership capability and demonstrated capability to grow within the organisational hierarchy, there is a clear message that gets imprinted into the culture that Leadership and related skills are not important for career growth. In the second chapter, we looked at having frameworks in place to ensure career planning is pegged to competencies in Leadership. This is essential. Unless these frameworks are in place, and are actually being made use of, career progression is pegged to either tenure and only to performance, and not to Leadership skills as well.

Another critical part is to ensure there is solid succession planning for critical Leadership positions. CEO transitions and CXO transitions need to be managed carefully, as having fundamentally different personalities and Leadership styles is quite the 'shock' to an organisation. There are certainly times when it is needed – especially in times of a turnaround. However, many times, Leadership positions are transitioned without taking into consideration Leadership attributes, which often spells disaster to otherwise well-functioning and growing organisations.

Organisations rely on key Leaders. Here are some examples:

- The Visionary Leaders – who are able to truly set direction, and also, very importantly, get everyone excited about the Vision.
- The Transformational Leaders/Change Champions – who are able to challenge the status quo and navigate change and transitions.
- The Inspirational Leaders – who uplift, inspire, create positivity and offer continuous hope.

- The Results-Oriented Leader – who drives performance and takes a hard-nosed, no-nonsense approach to performance and targets.
- The Technical Leader – who becomes the go-to person for technical solutions and related aspects.

Even though *all* Leaders are expected to be able to demonstrate these Leadership skills as and when required, it is often impossible to have all these skills and competencies in one person. Oftentimes, there are 'types' of Leaders – and each 'type' is required and needed for specific times of any organisation's trajectory and growth. Leadership, unlike a 'position' or 'title' is a 'role' individuals perform. This is why it is critically important to have 'Leadership succession' as much as 'succession planning' in the traditional 'hierarchical' or 'job role' perspective. Too many times, specific Leadership skills which are in a person are lost, and never quite replaced. The 'job' is filled, but the 'Leadership skills' are lost.

Janak Hirdaramani played a crucial role in the organisation being transformed from being a fledgling manufacturer of garments to the powerhouse it is today. His Vision, coupled with deep, sincere and genuine concern for people, won him deep love and adoration from an entire workforce who still speak of him with reverence and gratitude.

One of the stories Tony Nadaraja often shares is a shining example of the man Janak Hirdaramani was. The Maharagama plant was burnt to the ground during the 1983 communal riots – a dark moment in modern Sri Lankan history. The office functions moved to the head office, which was then situated in Fort.

Tony Nadaraja, then a Production Executive, was around when Janak said: 'We must pay our people'. When one of the three GMs said: 'But we have no records', Janak's classic reply was: 'You don't need records to pay. You need money. We will provide that.'

When someone asked: 'But how sir, all our records are burnt?', Janak's all time classic reply was: 'Advertise in the papers and radio, requesting everyone who worked to come to the Head Office. When they come, you ask them how much they got paid last, round it up and you pay that!'.

And that's exactly what they did. They paid every single employee full salary until they reopened manufacturing; purely based on the trust placed in them to tell the truth!

Whenever Tony tells this story, there is still that lump in his throat and tears visible in his eyes.

"THAT is the kind of man he was", is always the way he ends the story.

The difference between 'succession' and 'Leadership succession' cannot be better illustrated than through the transition of Janak Hirdaramani. When Janak Hirdaramani retired, his 'position' was filled by other family members and the next generation. The Hirdaramani Group still remains one of the most profitable (if not THE most profitable) groups on the island. His Vision and astute management practices were followed There is a delicate balance needed here. and continued, but what was never quite 'replaced' was that absolute, deep-seated and unwavering focus on people and their wellbeing. This was felt, often very significantly. It is true that an 'individual' cannot ever be replaced but their 'qualities' can be found in others – if you are aware of the need to develop them. Far too often we replace only 'the position', but not the characteristics and attributes of the incumbent!

Chapter 16

Retaining Leaders

You never stay only for the pay.
You never leave only because of the boss."

Retaining top talent is a huge topic of conversation within organisations and also, on a national level, in countries. As the world becomes more interconnected, and traditional jobs and work patterns continue to be disrupted over and over again, the need to retain the best personnel becomes far more important than ever, especially since many have far more choices in careers than they ever did.

Though the fundamentals of retaining anyone are argely the same, retaining Leaders needs to be identified a little differently.

First, you need to be able to 'spot' Leaders, as we have discussed. Simply spotting 'talent' per se isn't enough. You need to be able to spot Leaders and their innate Leadership capabilities and skills. Needless to say, once you have spotted Emerging Leaders, you need to continuously grow and develop them so that you are able to bring out their potential. Once Leaders are grown within the fold, and are contributing towards the organisation and Team positively, it is important to retain them.

A word of caution here. Retaining Leaders is not about selfishly keeping them within the fold, no matter what. Many times, Leaders outgrow the organisation, and when this happens, it is important to 'let them go' rather than stifling their growth. Trust and Loyalty go both ways; never forget that. So, as you watch Leaders grow, ensure you have an ongoing conversation about next steps, and if there is an indication to show that the Leader will outgrow the role, and the organisation is not able to offer them the opportunity for further growth and enhancement, discuss how an exit can take place with least impact to the organisation. This is why it is critical to have a succession plan in place for Leaders.

However, in a fiercely competitive marketplace, being able to retain your best Leaders IS important. Leaders are not the same as 'contributors' or 'individual performers'; they are a slightly different 'breed.'

Most Leaders, irrespective of their seniority within the organisation, share a few common traits which have a direct impact on how you need to focus on retaining them:

A. Most Leaders work for the personal challenge – not only for the money. They are driven by a sense of accomplishment and service. Most 'good' Leaders are often those who would consider being able to contribute and make a positive impact on others as important (if not more important) as their title, salary and other benefits. To retain them, you need to ensure they have a big enough challenge to truly get them excited.

B. Most Leaders are people-centric. Interacting, working with people and seeing them develop gives Leaders a sense of pride and accomplishment. Though there certainly are Leaders who are focused on technical aspects as well, most are people-centric above all else. So, to retain Leaders, you need to ensure their roles are centred around people.

C. Most Leaders are not simply 'compliant.' As they grow in confidence, it will become their second nature to challenge things and ask questions. To retain them, you need to have a culture which encourages open communication and also, the right to dissent.

D. Most Leaders have a rather strong moral compass. They understand the need for pragmatism and adaptability, but at the same time, they have certain values and principles that they are not willing to break or let go of. As such, organisations need to be careful in ensuring the cultural paradigms and structures are not divergent from that of the Leaders' values.

One of the other factors to consider is to have the ability for Leaders to work with other Leaders. Often, Leadership is seen as a singular activity rather than a collective activity. This gives rise to the 'celebration' of a 'person' or idolisation of an individual rather than the uplifting of a collective.

As much as there is focus on retaining the 'individual', understand that the collective that supports the individual is also important. Good Leaders have the ability to work with other Leaders, and often, there are informal 'cliques' of Leaders who come together to ensure work is done, and results achieved. So, when you are looking at retention, ensure you look at the impact of these 'informal networks' as much as looking at it from an individual's perspective.

Another important consideration in retaining Leaders is to understand what 'signals' you send when key Leaders leave. Someone leaving is inevitable – and often healthy. However, *how* they leave actually is more important than the leaving itself. Infighting, being disgruntled, losing faith in the overall ethos of the organisation as well as not buying into a new direction, these are all dangerous reasons for Leaders to leave, and when it happens it generally is not just attrition, it can lead to an exodus.

Be mindful that Leaders hold sway on opinion, and are often opinion Leaders. Seeing Leaders leave sends extremely negative signals to the rest of the organisation. So, be mindful that 'managing' Leader transits is important, and when people do leave, which is inevitable, it is not seen as a signal that the organisation is turning its back on its values, fundamental ethos or brand promise.

A wonderful example of Leaders being retained, but at the same time being given the opportunity to move out when they have outgrown the organisation is seen in the story of a client of ours who wished to remain anonymous. The organisation, within the highly competitive IT Industry, is small compared to most within the fold, but has a reputation for being able to attract as well as retain talent within its fold.

The founder and MD of the organisation has an annual 'touch base' with everyone who has been identified as potential Leaders of the future. He has detailed conversations with them on their aspirations, their insights into what needs to improve within the organisation, and also, about how they think they need to grow within the organisation. More than career progressions, which happen through a formal appraisal, the conversations are mostly about growth as an individual and a Leader – and notes are kept about each conversation. A follow-up happens after about six months. If anyone ever feels that they need to look out – for whatever reason, at the induction itself, the MD tells them that they should talk to him. He promises them NOT to challenge the decision but rather that he will use these insights to make sure the organisation becomes better. Many do take him up on it, and have a chat whenever they feel they are saturating and need to make a move. True to his word, he never tries to keep them back, but does offer them options of how he feels they can achieve bigger ambitions within the organisation. He also speaks to many of his peer CEOs/MDs and actively sends their CVs across, and the vast majority of individuals who have received 'breaks' in being offered professional positions owe thanks to him for opening doors for them. This has made him a truly trusted confidante, and many don't view him purely as their MD; rather, they see him as a person who will always do right by them.

This has built a reputation for the organisation as a place that is a wonderful place to come and learn, grow, and also, be assured that their best interests will always be safeguarded.

To this day, many who have left still talk fondly and appreciatively about the company they left and the Leader who put them first, always. This has also created a culture where all tiers of Leaders take on the same attitude, creating a truly great culture to grow Leaders at all levels.

Chapter 17

Retiring Leaders

"Too much of anything is good for nothing."

All careers come to an end: and Leaders are no different. No matter how successful they are, Leaders too must take their final bow and leave. When they do, ensuring there is no vacuum to fill is important. As discussed in *Chapter 15*, ensuring there is a solid success plan is critical.

Something to consider is that even in retirement Leaders can be, and often are, useful and value-adding. There is a deep tacit knowledge and an amazing depth of wisdom great Leaders have, and many times, we fail to tap into this when Senior Leaders retire. Sadly, we look at 'retirement' from their position and 'job', as a retirement from their role as a Leader as well. This is a mistake.

Again, there is a great parallel from traditional paddy cultivation to draw on. Many farmers work through into their 70s, some even longer. However, as they age, they are no longer able to be as efficient or effective in the field. When this happens, they instinctively hand over the 'reigns' of the 'chief farmer' role to one of their successors but continue to work the field, in a different capacity. He comes and observes the younger farmers, offers tips and hacks, helps the chief farmer with planning and organising and also, spends a lot of time looking at what can be improved. He takes the role of a mentor and Coach and plays a lesser role as a farmer, per se. Some continue to come to the field until they cannot physically walk any more. Their days are shorter – but they come, nonetheless. In some communities, there are groups of older farmers who come together to teach the younger farmers. They have informal sessions not only for farmers, but also for the blacksmiths on how to make better utensils, the wives about how to make sure the paddy is safeguarded from rats and other animals, and also become storytellers to the young ones, which often romanticises the life of a farmer, creating a longing to join in their ancestors' craft.

So, retired farmers perform three very important roles, long after they have stopped 'farming':

A. They Coach and mentor the new generation of farmers, and share wisdom, pass on tacit knowledge and invaluable insights and hacks.
B. They help build a community, act as agents who bring often conflicting groups together, and help smoothen things over when required.
C. They become evangelists for their trade.

A word of caution here, too. Extending retirement and getting Senior Leaders to perform the same function they used to because of their tacit knowledge is not what is expected here. In fact, *not* retiring individuals at the retirement age, no matter how good they are, is a clear sign of poor succession planning. It also creates a bad precedent and leads to inequity, as this cannot be extended for all concerned. However, using Leaders who retire to continue to perform coaching, mentoring, knowledge sharing and become 'storytellers' can and should be considered.

We observed this great practice in a school in Colombo. Teachers, Head Masters/Mistresses and Senior members of the academic staff were formed into a small 'Council of Elders' by the school. Through the Old Boys' Association, a small stipend was also given to them. Their role was simple: to come in 'ever so often' and observe, give guidance and advice and also, make recommendations.

This initiative took a life form of its own. Many turned up a lot more than 'ever so often' and became great Mentors and confidants for younger Teachers. They also gave much-needed insights to new Teachers who joined the school, and offered 'inside information' regarding students as well as fellow Teachers. Many of the younger members of the teaching fraternity 'consulted' the

'Council of Elders' (as they were affectionately known) about how to tackle especially boisterous classes, how to 'win over' some of their more challenging peers and also, how to change certain aspects of the organisation they felt needed change. Unencumbered with daily routines, chores or 'politics' the elders were able to offer great perspectives, whilst at the same time, being respectful of the culture and traditions of the school. They also met regularly with the administration and, while maintaining strict confidentiality, raised some of the common concerns they saw. They became a conduit to help the organisation improve.

Another important consideration is being able to give the retirees a proper 'send-off.' It is certainly not uncommon to have a small farewell party and give a retirement gift. However, it is important to make this event a celebration of what the individual stood for, as much as his/her contribution to the organisation. Make these events an opportunity to propagate values, and the role Leaders ought to play within the organisation.

Remember that you propagate what you celebrate. *Not* having a celebration for retirement is as bad as not doing it right. These events are symbolic – yes – but they send out very clear 'messages' to the employee population about who is celebrated and who is not. Having a major event for a hugely successful individual contributor who didn't live by company values and having a small one for a Leader who inspired and helped many is a clear message that 'performance' is respected and valued far more than 'Leadership.' So, be mindful that these are often not 'just events' to be managed, they are opportunities not to be missed.

One of the most touching 'send-offs' we witnessed was in a small manufacturing organisation on the retirement of their Chief Technician. By 'rank' he was way below the line and was not even in the 'executive[1]' grade. The individual who had worked for over 25 years within the organisation was considered a walking 'encyclopaedia' about his trade even though he was not formally 'qualified.' What made him so loved was that he was unselfish in imparting his knowledge and skills to any and all who came to him for guidance and help. A man with an amazing smile and a gentle demeanour about him, he was forever teaching someone.

1 Executive in Sri Lanka is not the same as an 'Executive' in the West. In Sri Lanka, Executive is below a Manager, and this is what most young graduates start off as. However, there is a 'non-executive' category in most manufacturing and related industries which are all the blue collar jobs belong to. Chief Technician is a level in the supervisory category, below the Executive tier.

His retirement 'event' was held in a 5-star hotel, and attended by the entire Management and Executive Teams. In the three-hour event before a gala dinner, a dozen people recited stories about how he had taught them, and helped them grow in their careers. The event, which was attended by his family as well, was something that resembled the Oscars.

The Chief Technician was not only given an official 'gift' but almost fifty employees came and gave a small personal memento to him. A small example of one was a framed handwritten note that gave technical details of a solution to a problem in a different section that a young engineer presented. The document was over fifteen years old, and the engineer was a Senior Manager now. He told the story of how he was struggling with an issue, and when he came to the 'Master' (as he was affectionately known) he had scribbled a solution and given him. The solution not only worked, but also got the young engineer on the 'radar' of the Senior Management.

He often consulted the Chief Technician for help – and every solution he offered was a hit. He told the audience about how he wanted to get the 'Master' promoted and come to his Team, and how he had politely refused, telling him that 'I am not an engineer' and you will need to 'break policy' if you get a non-qualified person promoted beyond his rank.

His selfless service was celebrated through the night, and many in the organisation told me that even Senior

Managers were never given a 'retirement party' this grand. It was very clear that the organisation truly recognised and celebrated this simple man's amazing Leadership qualities.

Epilogue

Over the past twenty years, much of my time has been spent in helping organisations train, coach and develop Leaders at all levels within their structures. Every time I start a new workshop, I always start with the same sentence:

'You can't train someone to be a Leader; you can only learn it. My job is to create an environment for you to learn how you can lead.'

One of the biggest challenges we have always had is convincing organisations that doing training Program after training Program is never enough to grow Leaders. We have had countless conversations about how we need to create ecosystems to ensure Leaders are grown at all levels within their organisation's fold. We have also had umpteen debates as to why Leadership development cannot simply be the domain of trainers and Coaches, and why it needs to be created through a collective, cohesive and holistic approach.

'Why don't you write a book on it, honestly?' one of my Clients told me, at the 'Big Match[1]' having a conversation over a beer. We were both a little too drunk, and I for one started laughing. He joined in the laughter after a while but insisted 'No, no, I know I am drunk, but I am serious, write a book on this.'

I forgot about it. But he didn't. He called me the Monday after and told me again.

'Machang, this whole thing of 'growing Leaders' is something that no one really gets. We all do training Programs, hoping that we develop Leaders, and you and I both know it doesn't work! So, do us a favour – and write a book on it – so that there can be a blueprint we can follow.'

So started the journey which sees its culmination today. After nearly three years of putting little notes together, collecting stories around best practices, and also, sifting through over twenty notebooks of notes from my training Programs and meetings, what I hope I have presented here is enough ideas and insights and illustrations to help

1 The 'Royal Thomian' Cricket Match (often referred to as the RoyTho) is possibly the longest continuous match being played on record and beats the 'ashes' in being played without a break for over 140 years. Those who have been to it will attest to the fact that the atmosphere and the revelry at the match is incomparable to any cricket match anywhere in the world. Part Mardi Gras, part a big fat Indian wedding and part Octoberfest, it is not to be missed if you are in Sri Lanka over March.

anyone develop a framework that will enable the growing of Leaders in their organisation.

Not offering a 'definitive framework' was intentional. I have always fought the urge to 'box things' and give 'one size fits all' type solutions. I have always held the notion that each organisation needs to evolve and grow their own frameworks. Simply 'copying' best practices and forgetting the contexts in which they worked is something I have always argued will never work. Building ecosystems requires spending time and energy in creating culturally fitting, authentic models, that become part of the organisation. Trying to 'transplant' practices or policy frameworks or processes often has counterproductive results.

As much as cultivating paddy in Thailand is different than in Sri Lanka, though the broad practices remain the same, growing Leaders needs to be something each organisation undertakes in their own right. What I hope this book offers is inspiration, ideas and also, concepts that will help you to do this.

Company Glossary

Bodyline (Pvt) Ltd.

https://www.masholdings.com/global-contact/sri-lanka/bodyline-sri-lanka/

Bodyline (Pvt) Ltd., a subsidiary of MAS Holdings, is a leading apparel manufacturer based in Sri Lanka. Established in 1992, the company specialises in the production of menswear, womenswear, and childrenswear for international markets. Bodyline is a significant player in the Sri Lankan apparel industry.

Industry/Sector: Apparel Manufacturing

Date Established: 1992

Key Milestones:

- 1992: Bodyline (Pvt) Ltd. was established as a subsidiary of MAS Holdings.
- 1994: Began operations with a focus on producing high-quality menswear for international markets.
- 2000s: Expanded product range to include womenswear and childrenswear.
- 2010s: Continued growth and expansion into new markets.
- 2022: Celebrated 30 years of operations with 30 corporate social responsibility (CSR) initiatives.

Brandix Lanka Limited

https://brandix.com/

Brandix Lanka Limited is a leading apparel manufacturer and exporter based in Sri Lanka, with a global workforce of over 60,000 associates. Since its establishment in 1972, Brandix has been a pioneer in the industry, achieving significant milestones in sustainability, innovation, and social responsibility. The company is committed to delivering high-quality products and services to its customers while minimising its environmental impact. Brandix has been recognized for its achievements through various awards and accolades, including being ranked among the top 10 most admired companies in Sri Lanka.

Industry/Sector: Apparel Manufacturing and Export

Date Established: 1972

Number of Employees: 60,000+ associates globally

Key Milestones:

- 1972: Founded as Phoenix Apparels Ltd.
- 1996: Became the first apparel manufacturer in Sri Lanka to receive ISO 9000 certification.
- 2002: Rebranded as Brandix Lanka Limited.
- 2007: Established the Brandix Green Factory, the first apparel factory in the world to be awarded the highest LEED Platinum rating.
- 2008: Launched the Brandix College of Clothing Technology.
- 2012: Became the first apparel company in Asia to be certified carbon neutral.
- 2018: Launched the Brandix i3 innovation center, focused on research and development in apparel technology.
- 2021: Ranked among the top 10 most admired companies in Sri Lanka.

CARE Sri Lanka

https://caresrilanka.org.uk/

CARE Sri Lanka was established in 1950 with a focus on food security and maternal and child health. Today, CARE works to address the root causes of poverty and marginalisation of vulnerable groups by building the skills of communities and promoting good governance within both government and community organisations.

Industry/Sector: International Non-Governmental Organisation (INGO)

Date established: 1950 (Globally); 1985 (In Sri Lanka)

Ceylon Biscuits Limited (CBL)

https://cbllk.com/

Ceylon Biscuits Limited (CBL) is a leading Sri Lankan food manufacturing conglomerate with a diverse product portfolio that includes biscuits, chocolates, cereal, cakes, and other convenience foods. Established in 1968, CBL has grown significantly over the years, expanding its product offerings and market reach. With over 6,000 Employees, the company is a major player in the Sri Lankan food industry and has a significant presence in international markets. CBL is committed to innovation and quality, consistently introducing new products and improving its existing offerings.

Date Established: 1968

Number of Employees: 6,000

Key Milestones:

- 1968: CBL commenced operations and created the protein-enriched Care biscuit to combat malnutrition in schoolchildren.

- CBL worked closely with communities to understand food needs.
- Today, CBL is a leading Sri Lankan food manufacturing conglomerate.
- CBL exports to over 65 countries.
- CBL has over 6,000 Employees.

Courtaulds Clothing Lanka (Pvt) Ltd.

https://www.srilankabusiness.com/exporters-directory/company-profiles/courtaulds-clothing-lanka-pvt-ltd/

Courtaulds Clothing Lanka (Pvt) Ltd. is a leading apparel manufacturer in Sri Lanka, established in 1998 as a subsidiary of the PD Enterprise Group. The company has a rich history, tracing its roots back to the original Courtaulds company founded in the United Kingdom in 1816. With over 10,000 Employees and ten manufacturing plants across Sri Lanka, Courtaulds Clothing Lanka is a significant player in the global apparel industry. The company is known for its high-quality garments and has established partnerships with some of the world's foremost retail clothing brands.

Industry/Sector: Apparel Manufacturing

Date Established: 1998 (in Sri Lanka)

Key Milestones:

- 1816: Courtaulds founded in the United Kingdom.
- 1998: Courtaulds Clothing Lanka established in Sri Lanka as a subsidiary of the PD Enterprise Group.
- 2000: Sara Lee Corporation acquired Courtaulds Textiles Plc, including the Courtaulds brand.
- 2006: Sara Lee Corporation spun off its branded apparel business, including the Courtaulds brand, as an independent company.

Dankotuwa Porcelain PLC

https://www.dankotuwa.com/

Dankotuwa Porcelain PLC is a Sri Lankan company specialising in the manufacture of porcelain tableware. The company was established in 1984 as a subsidiary of Ceylon Ceramics Corporation and was later privatized and listed on the Colombo Stock Exchange. Dankotuwa Porcelain is known for its high-quality products and has earned a reputation as one of the best in Asia and Europe.

Industry/Sector: Porcelain Tableware Manufacturing

Date Established: 1984 (as a subsidiary of Ceylon Ceramics Corporation)

Number of Employees: 1200+

Key Milestones:

- 1984: Incorporated as a subsidiary of Ceylon Ceramics Corporation.
- 1990: Privatised and subsequently listed on the Colombo Stock Exchange.
- 2010: Acquired by Environmental Resources Investment (currently known as Ambeon Holdings PLC).
- Awarded the "Most Loved Homeware Brand" in Sri Lanka by Brand Finance.
- Received the Gold Award at the 2020 NCE Export Awards in large-scale manufacturing in the porcelain and ceramics sector.
- Acquired by Ceyline Investments, a subsidiary of Ceyline Holdings, in July 2023.

GSK Sri Lanka

https://www.gsk.com/en-gb/locations/sri-lanka/

GSK Sri Lanka, established in 1939, is a subsidiary of the global biopharmaceutical company GSK plc, and it plays a significant role in the local healthcare sector. With a focus on innovation, GSK Sri Lanka is committed to improving the health of the Sri Lankan population through the provision of vaccines, specialty medicines, and consumer healthcare products. The company's local manufacturing facility in Ratmalana underscores its dedication to meeting local healthcare needs. Additionally, GSK Sri Lanka actively engages in community health Programs, contributing to the well-being of the community it serves. In 2023, GSK plc underwent a demerger, resulting in two independent companies: GSK, focusing on vaccines and specialty medicines, and Haleon, specializing in consumer healthcare.

Industry/Sector: Pharmaceuticals

Date Established: Presence in Sri Lanka for over 80 years,

Number of Employees: GSK global employee count is approximately 90,000+

Key Milestones:

- Local Manufacturing: Established a manufacturing facility in Ratmalana (year not specified on website).
- Focus on Innovation: Prioritizes research and development to bring innovative healthcare solutions to the Sri Lankan market.
- Community Engagement: Actively involved in community health Programs and initiatives.
- 2022: GSK plc demerged its consumer healthcare business into Haleon, leaving GSK focused on vaccines and specialty medicines

Hirdaramani Group

https://www.hirdaramani.com/

Hirdaramani is a global apparel manufacturer with a legacy dating back to 1890, starting with a retail clothing store in Colombo. The company has since expanded its operations across six countries and employs more than 55,000 associates. Hirdaramani is committed to sustainability, as evidenced by its achievement of net-zero emissions in its Sri Lankan apparel operations and its ambitious 'Future First' Sustainability Roadmap. The company is a pioneer in sustainable apparel manufacturing and continues to set the standard for ethical and environmentally responsible practices in the industry.

Industry/Sector: Apparel Manufacturing and Retail

Date established: 1890 (Retail); 1960s (Manufacturing)

Number of Employees: 55,000+ associates

Key Milestones:

- 1890: Parmanand Hirdaramani established the first retail clothing store in Fort, Colombo.
- 1940s: Hirdaramani Ltd. was established, pioneering the fashion retail industry with the introduction of 'Popular' and 'Diplomat' shirt brands.
- 1960s: Established Ceylon Knit Trend, the first export-scale factory, marking the beginning of large-scale apparel manufacturing in Sri Lanka.
- 2008: Opened Mihila, the world's first custom-built eco-friendly apparel factory, achieving LEED Gold certification.
- 2011: Mihila became Asia's first Carbon Neutral Apparel Factory.
- 2019: Achieved net-zero greenhouse gas emissions from energy use in Sri Lankan apparel operations.

- 2020: Achieved 40% sustainable sourcing.
- 2022: Launched 'Future First' Sustainability Roadmap 2025 with ambitious sustainability targets.

Jagro Fresh

http://www.jagrofresh.com/

Jagro Fresh, a subsidiary of CIC Holdings PLC, it's a Sri Lankan family-owned company not a subsidiary of CIC or any other 100% ownership in the family is a Sri Lankan company specialising in the cultivation, processing, and export of fresh strawberries and high-value vegetables. Established in 2003, Jagro Fresh is an ISO 22000 certified company committed to maintaining high-quality standards, sustainable agricultural practices, and ethical sourcing. The company serves both local and international markets, offering a wide range of fresh produce and value-added products. Jagro Fresh's commitment to quality, sustainability, and innovation has established it as a Leader in Sri Lanka's agricultural industry.

Industry/Sector: Agriculture, Food Processing, and Export

Date Established: 2003

Key Milestones:

- 2003: Jagro Fresh was founded, revolutionizing the local agriculture industry and changing its landscape.
- ISO 22000 Certification: Achieved ISO 22000 certification, operating under a stringent Food Safety Management System.
- Global G.A.P. Certification: First agricultural entity in Sri Lanka's fruit and vegetable sector to be certified in Global G.A.P.
- Sustainability Focus: Consistently incorporates best

practices into operations, minimising pesticide and fertilizer use, monitoring environmental impact, and following stringent quality management.

- Export & Retail: Supplies both local and overseas markets, wholesaling to modern trade and catering sectors, and retailing through a chain of owned cafes.
- Product Innovation: Engages in manufacturing strawberry jam and dessert topping with no artificial colors or flavours.

John Keells Holdings PLC (JKH)

https://www.keells.com/

John Keells Holdings PLC (JKH) is Sri Lanka's largest listed conglomerate, with operations spanning seven key sectors: Transportation, Consumer Foods & Retail, Leisure, Property, Financial Services, Information Technology, and Plantation Services. With over 13,000 Employees, JKH is a significant contributor to the Sri Lankan economy. JKH is committed to sustainability and social responsibility, and its John Keells Foundation actively supports community development Projects across the island. The company has a long and rich history of innovation, growth, and diversification.

Industry/Sector: Diversified Conglomerate

Date Established: 1870 (as a produce brokerage)

Number of Employees: 13,000+

Annual Earnings: LKR 265.78 billion (approximately USD 830 million in 2022)

Key Milestones:

- 1870: Founded as a produce and exchange broker by Edwin John.

- 1948: Merged with Anglo-Ceylon & General Estates Company Limited, entering the plantation sector.
- 1970s-80s: Expanded into the tourism and hospitality industry with the acquisition of several hotels.
- 1986: Listed on the Colombo Stock Exchange.
- 1991: Launched the Keells Super supermarket chain.
- 2000s: Diversified into other sectors such as financial services, information technology, and real estate.
- 2010s: Continued expansion and diversification, including the acquisition of Nations Trust Bank and the development of the Cinnamon Life Integrated Resort.
- 2022: Launched the John Keells X accelerator Program to foster innovation and entrepreneurship in Sri Lanka.
- 2023: The Group's transportation sector successfully concluded a landmark transaction with Adani Ports and Special Economic Zone Limited.

Maliban Biscuit Manufactories (Private) Limited

https://www.malibangroup.com/

Maliban Biscuit Manufactories (Private) Limited is a leading Sri Lankan biscuit manufacturer with a rich history dating back to 1954. The company offers a wide range of biscuits, crackers, cookies, and wafers, and is committed to providing high-quality products to consumers. Maliban has expanded its reach beyond Sri Lanka and now exports to over 35 countries. Throughout its history, Maliban has focused on innovation, quality, and customer satisfaction, solidifying its position as a trusted brand in the Sri Lankan and international markets.

Industry/Sector: Food Manufacturing (Biscuits and Confectionery)

Date Established: 1954

Key Milestones:

- 1954: Founded by A.G. Hinni Appuhamy.
- 1960s-70s: Expanded production capacity and product portfolio.
- 1980s: Introduced new product lines like Maliban Cream Cracker and Gold Marie.
- 1990s: Focused on modernization and automation of production facilities.
- 2000s: Expanded distribution network and increased exports.
- 2010s: Launched new products and entered new markets.
- Present: One of the leading biscuit manufacturers in Sri Lanka, with a presence in over 35 countries.

MAS Holdings

https://www.masholdings.com/

MAS Holdings is a global apparel-tech conglomerate, setting the industry benchmark for sustainable and ethical manufacturing. They are a leading concept-to-delivery solution provider in apparel and textile manufacturing, sought after by the world's leading brands.

Industry/Sector: Global Apparel-Tech Conglomerate

Key Milestones:

- 1985: Founded by Mahesh Amalean
- 1990: Began exporting apparel
- 2000: Opened first manufacturing facility in China
- 2010: Became the world's largest manufacturer of intimate apparel
- 2015: Launched MAS Innovation Lab
- 2020: Achieved carbon neutrality across its global operations

Methodist College, Colombo – *https://www.methodistcollege.lk/*

Methodist College, Colombo, established in 1866, is a prestigious private girls' school in Sri Lanka under the management of the Methodist Church. With a rich history spanning over 150 years, the school has consistently provided quality education and fostered a strong community of alumnae. The school's commitment to academic excellence, extracurricular activities, and character development has made it a leading educational institution in the country.

Industry/Sector: Education (Private School)

Date established: 1866

Number of people in employ: Approximately 75 teachers

Key Milestones:

- 1866: Founded as Kollupitiya Girl's English School by Miss Catherine Scott.
- 1883: Registered as a Grant-in-Aid English high school and renamed Kollupitiya Girls High School.
- 1915: Recognised as a fully organised Secondary School and renamed Methodist College.
- 1917: Establishment of the 1st Colombo (Methodist College) Guide Company.
- 1919: Formation of the Old Girls Association, which now has international branches.
- 1930: Introduction of the House system with four houses.
- 1950s: Expansion with the purchase of Framjee House and addition of two new houses.
- 1988: Inauguration of the Auditorium.

Mobitel

https://www.mobitel.lk/

With a history of over 163 years, SLT-MOBITEL is the National Information and Communications Technology (ICT) Solutions Provider, serving the nation's need for connectivity across fixed, mobile, and other operational segments. SLT-MOBITEL offers a range of ICT solutions that cater to consumers with a digital lifestyle, including Voice, Fiber, ADSL, 4G LTE, Cloud Services, Enterprise Solutions, wholesale, international ICT solutions, IPTV services, eChannelling, and a host of value-added services.

In its journey of transformation into a digital service provider, SLT-MOBITEL has expanded beyond ICT services to deliver products and services that leverage its core strengths, expertise, and assets. Positioned as a key global player, the company connects Sri Lanka to the world through international submarine cable systems. The group also offers submarine cable maintenance, Human Resources solutions, Directory services, Digital marketing solutions, and software solutions, among others.

With a strong local heritage, SLT-MOBITEL Mobile was the first network to launch the Super-3.5G HSPA network in South Asia in 2007 and subsequently trialed HSPA+, MIMO (Multiple Input Multiple Output) in 2009, another first in the region. SLT-MOBITEL Mobile went on to demonstrate 4G-LTE technology for the first time in South Asia in 2011 and trialed 4.5G LTE-Advanced Pro Technology with CA (Carrier Aggregation) of three bands.

In 2017, SLT-MOBITEL Mobile deployed the first Sub-1G Mobile Broadband Network in Sri Lanka based on a

900MHz spectrum to provide superior coverage to rural areas in the country. Continuing its Leadership, in 2018, SLT-MOBITEL Mobile launched the First Commercial 4.5G/4G+ Mobile Network in South Asia and successfully trialed 5G by connecting a commercial mobile smartphone to its 5G network. Furthermore, SLT-MOBITEL Mobile has been recognised by Ookla®, the global Leader in fixed broadband and mobile network testing applications, data, and analysis as the Fastest Mobile Network consecutively for 2019, 2020, and 2021. A growing customer base stands testament to SLT-MOBITEL's strong focus laid on National vision, Customer centricity, emulating its credo of 'The Connection.' For more information, visit www.sltmobitel.lk. Key Milestones:

- 1980: Formation of Sri Lanka Telecom Corporation
- 1993: Birth of Mobitel (Pvt) Ltd.
- 2002: Mobitel (Pvt) Ltd. became a fully owned subsidiary of Sri Lanka Telecom
- 2004: Launched its fully-fledged 2.5G GSM network that is EDGE/GPRS enabled and designed to operate on the dual band.
- 2007: first Mobile network to launch the Super-3.5G HSPA network in South Asia and subsequently trialed HSPA+, MIMO (Multiple Input Multiple Output) in 2009, another first in the region.
- 2011: Demonstrated 4G LTE for the first time in South Asia and Trialed 4.5G LTE-Advanced Pro Technology with CA (Carrier Aggregation) of three bands.
- 2017: SLT-MOBITEL Mobile deployed the first Sub-1G Mobile Broadband Network in Sri Lanka based on a 900MHz spectrum to provide superior coverage to rural areas in the country.

- 2018: SLT-MOBITEL Mobile launched the First Commercial 4.5G/4G+ Mobile Network in South Asia and successfully trialed 5G by connecting a commercial mobile smartphone to its 5G network.
- 2021: Brand Unification of Sri Lanka Telecom PLC and Mobitel forming 'SLT-MOBITEL' and The Connection that promised to revolutionize the telecom industry.

Pelemix

https://pelemix.com/

Founded in 1998 in Israel, Pelemix is a leading global provider of coir-based substrate solutions for professional growers and nurseries. With production facilities in multiple countries including Sri Lanka, India, Thailand, and Spain, Pelemix offers a diverse range of 100% natural coir products tailored to meet the specific needs of its customers. The company is committed to sustainability, providing eco-friendly cultivation options, and is recognized as a forerunner in the industry. In 2022, Pelemix was acquired by Sun Gro Horticulture, a leading provider of horticultural products in North America.

Industry/Sector: Coir-based Substrate Manufacturing and Distribution

Date Established: 1998

Founded in: Israel

Key Milestones:

- 1998: Founded in Israel, specializing in the production and marketing of Coco Coir and Coco Peat products and substrates.
- Global Expansion: Established production facilities in Sri Lanka, India, Thailand, and Spain.

- Product Innovation: Offers a wide range of 100% natural coir-based substrate products for professional growers and nurseries, including loose filled grow bags, compressed grow cubes, blocks, and open top grow bags.
- Customisation: Provides tailor-made substrate solutions to meet specific customer needs.
- Sustainability Focus: Promotes sustainable growth through eco-friendly cultivation options.
- Industry Recognition: Recognised as a forerunner in the coir substrate industry, serving customers across five continents.
- 2022: Acquired by Sun Gro Horticulture

Phoenix Industries Ltd.

https://www.phoenix.lk/

Phoenix Industries Ltd. is a leading Sri Lankan manufacturer of plastic and packaging solutions. The company has been at the forefront of the industry, continuously innovating and expanding its product portfolio. With a focus on quality, sustainability, and customer satisfaction, Phoenix Industries has become a trusted partner for businesses across various sectors.

Industry/Sector: Plastic and Packaging Manufacturing

Key Milestones:

- 1971: Established as a pioneer in Sri Lanka's plastic manufacturing industry.
- 1980s: Expanded into manufacturing industrial and consumer packaging solutions.
- 2000s: Diversified product portfolio to include PET preforms, closures, and injection-molded components.
- 2010s: Expanded production capacity with new state-of-the-art facilities.

- 2020: Launched a new factory in Horana, purpose-built to deliver just-in-time packaging for Unilever.

Raheema Hotel and Stores Pvt Ltd. – *https://rainbowpages.lk/other/branches/raheema-hotel-and-stores-pvt-ltd-colombo-07/*

Raheema Hotel and Stores Pvt Ltd. is a restaurant chain operating in Colombo, Sri Lanka, specializing in Sri Lankan and Asian cuisine. With a multi-branch presence, it caters to a diverse customer base. It offers a range of dishes and provides delivery services. The company maintains an online presence across platforms like TripAdvisor, Rainbow Pages, and Top Rated Online.

Industry/Sector: Hospitality (Restaurant)

Key Features:

- Established Presence: Operates multiple branches in Colombo (03 and 07)
- Menu Offerings: Offers a variety of Sri Lankan and Asian cuisine
- Delivery Services: Provides delivery services through platforms like Uber Eats.
- Online Presence: Listed on various online platforms like TripAdvisor, Rainbow Pages, and Top Rated Online.

S. Thomas' College, Mount Lavinia – *https://www.stcmount.edu.lk/*

S. Thomas' College, Mount Lavinia, is a leading private Anglican boys' school in Sri Lanka. Founded in 1851, it has a long and distinguished history of providing quality education to generations of Sri Lankan students. The school is known for its strong academic tradition, as well as its emphasis on extracurricular activities such as sports, music, and drama. S. Thomas' College has produced many notable alumni who have gone on to make significant contributions in various fields. The school continues to be a sought-after institution for boys' education in Sri Lanka. S. Thomas' College, Mount Lavinia is also the author's alma mater.

Industry/Sector: Education (Private School)

Date Established: 1851

Key Milestones:

- 1851: Founded by Bishop James Chapman, the first Bishop of Colombo.
- 1854: Moved to Mutwal.
- 1923: Moved to Mount Lavinia, its current location.
- 1951: Celebrated its centenary.
- 1980s: Introduced the G.C.E. Advanced Level curriculum.
- 2001: Celebrated its 150th anniversary.

Slimline Pvt Ltd. (a subsidiary of MAS Holdings) – *https://www.slimlineparanakela.com/slimline.php* and *https://www.masholdings.com/global-contact/sri-lanka/*

Slimline Pvt Ltd., initially incorporated in 1993 as a joint venture between Courtaulds PLC (UK), MAST Industries (USA) and MAS Holdings (Sri Lanka) – was later bought by MAS in 2006, and is now a flagship manufacturing facility within the MAS Holdings.

Now known as Unichela Pvt Ltd – Slimline division, Slimline specializes in intimatewear and athleisure. Since its establishment in 1993, the company has grown to become a major supplier for global brands like Victoria's Secret. Slimline is committed to sustainable practices and has received recognition for its efforts, including LEED Platinum certification for its eco-friendly factory.

Industry/Sector: Apparel Manufacturing

Date Established: 1993

Number of People in Employ: over 4,000 people

Key Milestones:

- 1993: Slimline was founded as a joint venture
- 1996: Specialised in intimate wear manufacturing for Victoria's Secret

About the Author

Vidusha is a HR Consultant and Leadership Trainer based out of Sri Lanka. For over two decades, Vidusha has conducted training and consulting assignments across 15 countries in person, with participants from over 30 countries online. His work in creating a framework to assess validated ROI after training was one of the first frameworks around linking Leadership Training and ROI, and won him a place on the TedX Colombo stage.

Vidusha has won many recognitions over the years for his pioneering work in the Leadership space, including being the only Sri Lankan to be in the Top 50 Leadership Thought Leaders in Global Gurus, as well as being identified as one of the Top 30 Global Thought Leaders in Management and Leadership by Thinkers 360. Vidusha has over 70 self published books – all of which are available for free (honouring a commitment he made to his father not to 'sell' books he writes) on www.booksbyv.com. This is the same reason all proceeds from this book too will go directly to charity.

Vidusha is also one of the two Founding Directors of Chrysalis – a social enterprise and a CARE affiliate, working on empowering women and youth, and fostering micro entrepreneurs across Sri Lanka.

He headed the HR and HRD functions for the local arm of a Fortune 500 company before moving into consulting and training. He was the youngest Head of HR for the Group to date, and won several accolades for innovative HR practices, including being part of the team that won the National Safety Awards for 3 years, the National Energy Saving Award for 2 years, and the First Runner Up Award for the inaugural HR Awards in Sri Lanka. His team also achieved the monumental achievement of 10 million clock hours without a lost time accident – one of very few organisations across the global group to achieve this feat!

Vidusha holds a Bachelors in Business from the University of Lincoln (UK), an MA in Leading Innovation and Change from the University of York, St. John (UK), an MBA from the University of Wales Trinity St. David and an MA in HR from the University of Northampton. He is currently reading for his PhD, for which he is researching the role that power plays in the emergence of Collective Leadership.

Vidusha lives in Kandy, in a veritable jungle, preferring to take a step back from the 'rat race', and spend a bit more quality time with his family. He has a daughter and a son, and pays tribute to his wife for inspiring him to start on his own. In his free time, Vidusha loves to embark on adventures, and recently climbed Mt. Kilimanjaro with his teenage son. He has also paddled most rivers across the island. Vidusha also writes a lot of poems and short stories in Sinhala, his native language.

www.ingramcontent.com/pod-product-compliance
Lightning Source LLC
Chambersburg PA
CBHW070756270326
41927CB00010B/2164